The 11-
a practical
guide for
parents

by

Mark Chatterton
(MA Oxon)

HADLEIGH BOOKS

© HADLEIGH BOOKS 2015

PAPERBACK BOOK VERSION – ISBN 978-1-910811-13-9

First published in Great Britain in 2015 by

Hadleigh Books
Church Road
Hadleigh
Essex
SS7 2HA
United Kingdom

www.hadleighbooks.co.uk

Disclaimer: All the text inside this book is for information purposes only. The author and Hadleigh Books cannot accept any responsibility for any inaccuracies or errors within the text, or loss, injury or inconvenience resulting from the use of information contained in this guide. Every effort has been made to check that this book is as up-to-date as possible at the time of publication. Please note that grammar and other schools do change the date of their 11+ test from time to time, as well as the subjects taken and other aspects of their admissions procedures. Always check with the individual grammar schools and local authorities for the most up to date information. Any grammar or other school mentioned by name in the text is purely for illustrative purposes only and neither the author nor Hadleigh Books have any connection with those schools.

Front cover designed by Ian Jones of UberMagicTwo Ltd
www.indigosites.co.uk

Introduction

It could be argued that the 11+ exam is the one exam which causes more upset, anguish and worry than any other exam. Not just to the students, but also to the parents! The words, "minefield" and "maze" are two that are often used by worried parents, who are faced with the prospect of their son or daughter taking the 11+ exam for the first time.

Nowadays the 11+ exam and all it entails has become a multi million pound industry. For example, there are now over thirty different companies in Britain who publish 11+ practice papers. Then there is the phenomenal growth of private tutors, tutor agencies and tutor centres, as well as the introduction of "Mock 11+ test days". Finally in recent years we have seen the arrival of psychological counselling for some children, (not to mention the parents!) who get stressed by it all.

When I first got involved with the 11+ as a primary school teacher over twenty years ago, virtually none of this happened. The children took the exam in their own primary or prep school in familiar surroundings. There was usually just one subject they were tested in, which was Verbal Reasoning. The test papers were marked within twenty four hours by their own teachers in their own school. We also gave a grade of what we thought the child's ability was. The grammar school then decided whether to give a place to each child based on our recommendations and how well they did in the test. Also the primary schools were warned that if they were found coaching the children beforehand, their place would be withdrawn and be given to someone else!

Oh how times have changed......

The purpose of this book is to help parents see what is involved in the 11+ exam in the twenty first century. I have tried to make this book as practical as possible. So I have covered every conceivable angle that the 11+ exam has. For instance, how does the 11+ work in practice? What is the child expected to do to prepare for the exam? How should the parents support their children through this often daunting hurdle in their lives? What subjects are taken in the 11+? Where are the grammar schools situated? What are the different types of grammar schools? What are the alternatives to taking the 11+, especially if my child does not make the grade? How do you apply for the 11+? How do I appeal if my child is not successful? Plus I have included several useful hints and tips for the children in both preparing for and in taking the 11+ exam itself.

As, I mentioned earlier, many parents see the 11+ as a minefield, so hopefully by reading this book, both you and your child will make the journey through the 11+ safely and successfully.

Mark Chatterton

May 2015

Acknowledgements

The author would like to thank the following parents for their advice, suggestions and help in creating this book:-

Adele Rogers, Lisa Rogers, Jo Lineham, Janette Topel

About the author

Mark Chatterton has over twenty years experience of preparing children for the 11+ exam. He has taught in both state and independent schools and is a graduate of Oxford University and a member of Mensa. He is the founder of the 11 Plus website and the Education website. He has also written several volumes of 11+ practice papers which are published by MW Educational. All three of his children took the 11+ exam and went onto grammar schools.

Please note

Neither Mark Chatterton nor Hadleigh Books are able to answer any questions about the 11+ personally. If there is anything that you have not been able to find the answer to in this book, please contact your local education authority or grammar school for more information.

CONTENTS

CHAPTER 1 – AN OVERVIEW OF THE 11+ EXAM

In this chapter I give an overview of the 11+ exam, explaining what it is, how it works and how grammar schools use it.

What is the 11+ exam?

The "11 Plus" or "11+" is a selective examination which is set by state grammar schools in England. It is seen as a way for the grammar schools to decide which children are suitable to enter their schools in Year 7, based on the score they achieve in the test. It does not take place everywhere in England, but only in areas where there are grammar schools. It is called the 11+ as that is the age at which children will be when they enter their secondary schools. This is despite the fact that the vast majority of children are actually ten years old when they take the 11+ exam. In some areas it is known as the "Transfer Test".

The 11+ exam came into force in Britain in 1944 with the passing of the Education Act (also called "The Butler Act") and stayed that way until the 1960's. In this decade the Labour Government of the day brought in large scale changes to Secondary education in Great Britain. The most far reaching of these was the introduction of the Comprehensive system of Secondary education. This resulted in many councils abolishing their grammar schools and turning them into comprehensive schools, where no selection test was needed for entry. Some English councils however, chose to keep their grammar schools and these are still in existence today. No Welsh or Scottish councils kept their grammar schools, so that is why there are no grammar schools in Wales or Scotland. In Northern Ireland, where the 11+ exam was phased out in 2008, most secondary schools still have a selection test for pupils entering their schools, which is similar in style to the old 11+ exam.

Just to confuse things, some other types of schools (which can either be state comprehensives or private secondary schools) also have their own version of the 11+. This is also a selection test, which they set as a way of seeing which pupils they will accept, when there are more applicants than places available.

Where does the 11+ for grammar school entrance take place?

The English counties and metropolitan boroughs which still have state grammar schools are :- Berkshire, Birmingham, Bristol, Buckinghamshire, Cheshire, Cumbria, Devon, Dorset, Essex, Gloucestershire, Hertfordshire, Kent, Lancashire, Lincolnshire, Liverpool, London, Manchester, Medway, Middlesex, North Yorkshire, Shropshire, Surrey, Warwickshire, West Midlands, West Yorkshire and Wiltshire.

Please note that you do not get grammar schools in every town in the areas mentioned above. For example in the county of Essex, there are grammar schools in the towns of Southend and Colchester, but not in those of Harlow or Basildon.

There is more information on grammar schools in the next chapter.

How does the 11+ exam work?

As places at the existing grammar schools are in high demand, the only way of securing a place, is by your child reaching a high enough mark in the 11+ selection test, which each grammar school sets. Estimates say that roughly 100,000 children sit the 11+ exam in England each year for around 15,000 places, giving each child a 1 in 6 chance of gaining a place. In some areas where demand is even greater, the odds are a 1 in 10 chance of passing the 11+. So you can see that gaining a place in a state grammar school is a huge achievement for those who are successful.

When does the 11+ exam take place?

The date of a particular 11+ selection test to a grammar school varies from area to area, but generally speaking most state grammar schools have their entrance tests in the months of September and October, when the children are in Year 6 of primary school. For example, schools in Essex and Lancashire hold their tests in September, whilst those in Surrey and Yorkshire hold their test days in October. There are even some grammar schools in the Wolverhampton and Shropshire areas that now hold their test days in July. So in practise the children in these areas are actually taking the 11+ test when they are in year 5 and still aged nine in some cases! Whether this will influence other schools to do the same, remains to be seen.

If you are applying to an independent grammar school, their test days may be much later in the school year, such as January or March. The important thing is to make sure you know when the test date is for each particular grammar school you are applying for and when the closing date for your application is.

There is a whole chapter on the application process later on in this book.

What subjects are set in the 11+ exam?

The subjects which are set in the 11+ exam vary from area to area. However the 11+ exam usually consists of one or more of these four subjects:-

English, Mathematics, Non-verbal Reasoning, Verbal Reasoning.

For example at the time of writing, in Lincolnshire children are tested in the subjects of Non-Verbal Reasoning and Verbal Reasoning. Whilst those sitting the 11+ in Wiltshire, are tested in the subjects of English, Maths and Verbal Reasoning. So each area is different and you as a parent will need to check with each grammar school(s) you are applying for which subjects are set.

Below are details of the subjects your child will usually have to attempt in the 11+ exam. I have added some more detailed sample questions in all four subjects for you to see the scope and level of difficulty.

English - In 11+ English there is usually a comprehension paper where a passage of text or information is set with several questions based on the passage. Also expect questions based on punctuation, parts of speech and English grammar. In some areas the pupil may have to write an essay or a short piece of writing.

Here are a couple of sample English questions:-

Example 1: Based on a passage of comprehension, a typical question might be like this:-

What does "disposal" (line 22) mean in this context?

(a) Opportunity   (b) Use   (c) Freedom   (d) Waste

Answer: b (use)

Example 2: In the sentence below a noun has been written before a sentence. Change the noun into an adjective and write the new word on the line provided:-

Circle   -   I created a _____ pattern in the book.

Answer: circular

Mathematics – Most 11+ Maths papers test the child on all aspects of Maths including the four rules (addition, subtraction, multiplication and division), fractions, percentages, shape, area, graphs, money, measurement, problem solving and time. Some questions will be digit based, whilst others will be written problem type Maths questions

Here are a couple of sample Maths questions:-

Example 1: If $W = 2$, $X = 5$, $Y = 10$ and $Z = 20$, work out this letter sum. Write your answer as a LETTER.

$Y + (X \times W) =$ _____

The answer is: Z (5 x 2 = 10. 10 + 10 = 20. 20 as a letter is Z) If a child put 20 as an answer it would be marked wrong, as they hadn't followed the instructions in the question to write the answer as a letter.

Example 2: If a plane travelled at an average speed of 800 km per hour on a journey that started at 08.00 hours and finished at 11.30 hours, how far was its journey?

Answer: 2,800 km. The total journey time was 3 hours 30 minutes or 3.5 hours (11.30 minus 08.00). Multiply 3.5 by 800 and you get 2,800)

Non-verbal Reasoning - The 11+ Non-verbal Reasoning test does not have any written questions, but instead has logic type questions based on shape, patterns, numbers, symmetry and sequences.

Here are a couple of sample Non Verbal Reasoning questions:-

Example 1: In the four boxes on the left you can see that there is a box that is blank. Work out which of the five boxes on the right contains the correct missing shape or object so that there is a sequence.

6)

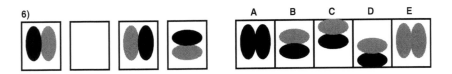

The answer is B, as the shapes all turn in an anticlockwise direction and are not touching the sides of the box. Plus there is one grey coloured oval and one black coloured oval in each box.

Example 2: In each line below there are five boxes with various symbols and shapes in them. Four of the five boxes have something that connects them, whilst one of the boxes contains something that makes it different to the other four. Work out which box is the odd one out.

6)

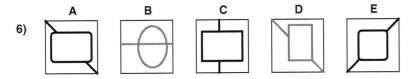

The answer is B, as it has a line cutting across the top of the shape, whilst the others all have lines which go behind the shapes.

Verbal Reasoning - There are around twenty possible types of questions used in 11+ Verbal Reasoning tests throughout England. These may include letter and number sequences, analogies, letter and number codes, spotting the odd one out, words which come in the middle of a certain group, word endings/beginnings and anagrams.

Here are a couple of sample Verbal Reasoning questions:-

Example 1: In each line below, you have to work out what the next two pairs of letters in the letter sequence will be. Write your answers on the lines provided:-

BC   FG   JK   NO   ___   ___

The answer is: **RS** and **VW**. (You miss out the next two letters in alphabetical order in between each pair of letters). Please note if a child got one pair correct and one pair wrong they wouldn't receive a half mark. Instead the answer would be marked wrong as they would be expected to get both pairs of letters correct to receive the mark.

Example 2: If Song B enters the music charts three places above Song A that had dropped five places from the number two slot the previous week, at what position in the charts is Song B?

Answer: Number four. (Song A goes down five places from number 2 so it is now number 7 in the new chart. So if Song B is three places above that, it will be at number 4).

These examples are just a fraction of the different types of questions set in the 11+ exam, which will vary from area to area. Please be aware that the standard of questions in the 11+ will be harder than the usual year 6 questions set in tests such as the SATs.

Tip: In order to get an idea of what the 11+ questions are like, you could put an internet search in your computer for "free 11+ tests", or "11 plus question examples". These are free, as many educational publishers now provide free 11+ questions or tests as a way of attracting potential customers to their websites. Also some grammar and private schools do have past papers on line for you to download for free in some cases. Try searching for "past 11+ papers" and see what comes up.

The difference between 11+ standard format versions and 11+ multiple choice format versions

To further complicate things, the way the child answers the 11+ questions can vary from area to area. Basically there are two versions of answering the questions in the 11+. These are "Standard" format and "Multiple Choice" format. In the early years of the 11+, the tests were of the "standard" type, whereby the child would write down an answer to a particular question on the paper, purely by working out the answer by themselves. Or s/he would underline a particular answer from a line of possible answers.

Increasingly, several grammar schools (such as the ones in Kent and Buckinghamshire) have brought in multiple choice format tests. With this format the child is given a choice of four or five possible answers for each question, usually in a box. S/he must then choose the one answer that they think is correct. They do this usually by drawing a horizontal line through a box next to the answer, rather like the National Lottery slip, or in some cases filling in the box.

Here are two examples of these:-

or

This is the main type of multiple choice answer question box used in the 11+, though some 11+ tests now have this version below:-

E.g. How many times did Adam knock on the door? Tick one box only.

1) once

2) twice

3) He didn't knock at all

In the example above the child needs to put a tick in one of the boxes instead of a horizontal line. Please be aware that some questions might ask you to tick two or even three boxes for your answer.

So there are basically two different types of multiple choice answer formats, which will vary according to which area your child sits the 11+ in. The idea of having them is that they can be marked by scanning the sheets into a computer as opposed to a human being manually marking them, which can be both quicker and cheaper for the school concerned.

There are pros and cons with both standard and multiple choice formats. Many argue that the standard version gives the examiner a truer picture of the child's ability as it is 100% from the child. On the other hand multiple choice answers already have the answer there in front of you and it is possible for a child to "second guess" the answer, even if he or she doesn't actually know the answer. So it may not show a true picture of the child's ability. At the moment multiple choice version 11+ tests seem to be on the increase, not least because of the ease in marking them.

Who sets the questions in the 11+?

This where it gets confusing! For many years the 11+ exam was set by an independent educational organisation called the National Foundation for Educational Research – "NFER" for short. They set the 11+ tests for virtually all the grammar schools and many independent schools as well. They were known as NFER Nelson until 2000 when they were sold to

Granada Learning. In 2007 the name was changed to GL Assessment, which is the current provider and publisher of 11+ tests used by many grammar schools.

However in 2013, several grammar schools started using 11+ tests set by an organisation known as CEM, or the Centre for Evaluation and Monitoring, based at Durham University. The big idea that sprang up around the CEM tests was that they were "tutor proof", i.e. children couldn't be tutored to pass these tests as they wouldn't know what types of questions would come up. Although some parents and tutors, as well as plenty of educational publishers, would argue that this isn't the case, an increasing number of grammar schools are choosing to use these papers in favour of the GL Assessment ones.

In some areas, notably Hertfordshire, some schools use 11+ exam papers set by Moray House, based at Edinburgh University, though these are only a small percentage of all grammar schools.

Finally, some of the grammar schools themselves write their own 11+ exams. These might be just the Maths or English papers, whilst they will still use Verbal Reasoning from GL Assessment or CEM. The Essex Consortium of Grammar Schools has for many years used its own written exams for the 11+ entrance exam in the subjects of English and Mathematics. Since 2014 it stopped using NFER Verbal Reasoning as a test subject and so may be the only set of grammar schools to completely use its own questions. This could well be the start of a trend that other areas will follow. Watch this space!

What is the pass mark in the 11+?

Whenever parents ask me "What is the pass mark for the eleven plus?" I usually reply, "There isn't one!" By this I mean there isn't a pass mark per se, such as 80%. If the grammar schools set a pass mark such as this, what would happen if two hundred pupils reached this pass mark when there were only one hundred places available? Rather the "pass mark" for each grammar school will vary each year, according to the mark the hundredth child achieved in getting that last place available. What that means is that if the hundredth child attained a score of 75% overall, that would be the "pass mark" for that particular year's entry group. If in the next year the hundredth pupil achieved a score of 85%, then that would be the pass mark for that year's entry group and the level of difficulty of the subjects set. Perhaps the term "bench mark" might be better here because the standard needed to gain entry to each grammar school will always vary year by year according to several factors, including the calibre of the pupils in one particular year group However this "raw score" as it is known is just one of several factors that are used in determining a child's score in the 11+ exam. There are one or two other factors which come into play, including the complicated "standardised score". I will now explain about this.

Standardised Scores

The main thing that parents need to know about pass marks for the 11+ exam is that each child is given a "score", which is not just an average of the number of tests they take, but is also age standardised. This standardised score is the actual final mark, or "score" the pupil is given in the 11+ exam. How it is worked out is quite complicated, but in simple terms a mark of 100 is used as the average for the whole group taking the 11+ test. So the lowest mark is usually around 70 and the highest about 130, though this may be lower or higher.

If two children took the test with birthdays in September and August, the one born in September would be at an age advantage having covered more of the curriculum over his/her lifetime, as opposed to the August born child. To counteract this, the scores are standardised to make things equal and fair for both children. It doesn't mean that the September born child loses marks and the August born child gains marks. It means rather, that factors such as age, how difficult the test is, how bright the group taking the test is, etc, are all taken into account when working out this score.

So when a child is given his/her score for the 11+, the cut off score might be 120 or 130 depending on the standard of the test that particular year.

To confuse you even further, some grammar schools do not use this score for their system, but instead have one where the score is in the 200s or 300s! So a cut off mark for the 11+ might be 300 one year and 310 another. Then again the score might be even higher for children who are not living within a particular grammar school's catchment area, say 330 for example.

What you as a parent need to check is the mark/score that is needed as the cut off/pass mark for each particular grammar school you are interested in. Usually this can be found on the grammar school's website. Alternatively your local authority or child's head teacher should be able to give you this information.

Tip: To get a more detailed idea of how standardised scores are worked out, try looking up "11+ standardised scores" on the internet and then the name of the grammar school.

When are the results of the 11+ published?

This varies according to the grammar school, but since 2013, the results for the 11+ tend to come out sometime during the month of October. Some schools do publish them earlier than this, though they are a minority. They come out so early in the school year as parents have to apply to the local authority with their choices of Secondary school by 31st October.

In the letter or e-mail from the grammar school, you will not be told if your child has "passed" or "failed" the 11+. Instead you will be told his or her score in the 11+ exam and the minimum score needed to secure a place at that particular grammar school. In many ways this system is fairer on the child taking the 11+, as the words "pass" and "fail" are no longer used. It is only the parents who seem to use these terms nowadays. I still get parents coming up to me who say, "I failed the 11+" - an event which happened twenty of thirty years ago in their lives, yet this still affects them in some way. Hopefully the new system will not leave such a psychological mark on the children who take the 11+ today.

Once you know whether your child has reached the required score or not for a grammar school, you are in a better position to make your choices for all the secondary schools in your area. Since 2004 the name of the secondary school your child has been offered a place at, is sent out on 1st March - National Results Day. (If this occurs on a weekend day, the following Monday is deemed to be National Results Day). You can choose to be told your results by e-mail or post. (Obviously some letters arrive sooner than others depending on the post). You will then have around two to three weeks to decide whether you are going to accept or reject the secondary school that your child has been allocated. This is the stage at which you can appeal against the decision if you wish to do so. You can also ask to be put on a certain school's waiting list as well. I will go into this subject in more detail later on in the book. However your local education authority will be able to give you more details about how this procedure is carried out in your local area.

How can I apply for my child to sit the 11+ exam?

This is quite a complicated process and I will go into this in more detail in the coming chapters, so keep reading!

In the next chapter I will look in more detail about grammar schools, such as why they are so popular, how the name "grammar" can be confusing and what type of education you would expect your child to get in a grammar school.

CHAPTER 2 – GRAMMAR SCHOOLS AND WHY THEY ARE SO POPULAR WITH PARENTS

If you are thinking of putting your child in for the 11+ exam to enter a grammar school, it is important that you understand what the term, "grammar school" actually means, as well as the ethos of a grammar school. Let's start with the definition of what a grammar school actually is and how they developed over time.

What exactly is a grammar school?

To understand this question, you need to go back in time to see how grammar schools have evolved to what they are today. The term "grammar school" dates back to before the Middle Ages when the first grammar schools were founded. (The earliest recorded grammar school is believed to be Thetford Grammar School, which was founded in 631). These were schools for boys who were expected to go into the priesthood, and as such were attached to religious institutions like monasteries and cathedrals. Initially they were taught the classical languages of Latin and Greek. Emphasis was placed on the learning of the grammar side of these languages; hence the name "grammar school" came to be used to describe these places of learning.

As time went on, more and more grammar schools were founded by rich benefactors and more subjects were added to the curriculum. By Victorian times there were over a thousand grammar schools in existence, all educating boys. In addition to the grammar schools, "public schools" had started to become popular as an alternative type of school. These included Eton, Westminster and Rugby Schools. They were essentially boarding schools where parents paid for the privilege of a private education.

At this stage, the education of girls was a long way behind that for boys. It wasn't until the late nineteenth century and the early twentieth century that secondary education for females took off, with the introduction of "high schools" for girls. These weren't called grammar schools as such, but were of a similar ethos and curriculum.

The 1944 Education Act

Gradually the way schooling had evolved in Britain over time had resulted in a hotchpotch of different types of schools, which called for huge reforms. These eventually came in the 1944 Education Act, whose architect was the educationalist R.A.B. Butler. Schooling in the United Kingdom was rearranged so that children would be entitled to free education between the ages of 5 and 15. Thus children aged 5-11 would attend a primary school, and children aged 11-15 would attend a Secondary school.

From this time onwards there would be three types of Secondary schools - Grammar Schools, Secondary Modern Schools and Technical Schools or Colleges. This came to be known as the "Tripartite System".

Each school was designed to fit in with the child's educational capabilities. So a grammar school would suit those who were academic and wanted to go onto university; whilst a Technical School suited those who wished to pursue a trade, with a Secondary Modern fitting somewhere in between. All children took the 11+ exam in their final year of primary school and based on their performance in this exam; they would then go onto one of these three types of secondary school.

There were two types of grammar school at this time. The majority were maintained grammar schools, where their funds came entirely from the state. The minority were direct grant grammar schools, where over half of the pupils were fee-paying, whilst the rest of the pupils received a grant from the government to pay their fees.

The ending of the Tripartite System

This system was in place for the next twenty years or so, but as time went on, many politicians and educationalists felt that this system was not fair on the less academic children. For example they felt that local education authority funding was biased towards the grammar schools and so by the 1960's the then Labour Government decided to bring in a comprehensive system of education. The idea was to abolish the three school system and introduce a more "comprehensive" system where all children were to be treated fairly and would all attend the same type of secondary school. Children would no longer have to take the 11+ examination to see which secondary school they would go to.

This meant that by the 1970's the number of Grammar Schools declined rapidly to be replaced by Comprehensives. The speed of this change varied from local authority to local authority as there was no set time limit for this process to happen. Some grammar schools elected to become private grammar schools, some changed to comprehensives and some remained as grammar schools. This latter group is where the 11+ exam is still used today as a means of entry.

In 1997 when the new Labour government was elected, a law was introduced which allowed parents from an area where there was a grammar school to vote for the abolition of the local grammar school. Although a few referenda did take place, none of them succeeded in their aim and so grammar schools still remain in a strong position today with strong parental support in their favour. Grammar schools invariably do well in the League Tables for secondary schools and their Ofsted reports are usually very impressive.

What happens in Scotland, Wales and Northern Ireland?

In Scotland the secondary schooling system is different as all secondary schools became comprehensives by the end of the 1970s. These usually have the title "Academy" or High School" attached to their name. Just to confuse things, there are some Scottish secondary schools which still have the title "Grammar" in their name, such as "Aberdeen Grammar", or "Lanark Grammar", even though they are comprehensive in system. In Wales all grammar schools were also phased out by the end of the 1970's. Northern Ireland however is different and has kept the majority of its grammar schools in place, with an 11+ exam taking place whilst the primary pupils are in Year 7, the final year of primary education in Northern Ireland. This system lasted until 2008 when the 11+ exam was discontinued by law, though it seems to have resurfaced in another form, with the majority of secondary schools opting for an 11+ type selection test to be taken whilst the children are in year 7.

Tip: If you are a parent based in Northern Ireland, it would be prudent to visit the two websites of the two organisations who deal with the selection process in Northern Ireland, post 2008, for more information. These are:
The Association of Quality Education - http://aqe.org.uk/
The Post Primary Transfer Consortium - http://www.pptcni.com/

So the term "Grammar School" can mean several types of school?

This can all get quite confusing! Basically any secondary school can be called "grammar school" in its name, due to historical reasons. So it could be a comprehensive, a private school, or what parents would term a "grammar school" in the traditional sense. That is a state school which uses the grammar school system of education and accepts pupils through the 11+ exam.

Let's look at these in more detail.......

Group 1 – These are comprehensive schools which have continued to use the term "grammar school" in their school's name. When they changed from a grammar school to a comprehensive school in the nineteen sixties/seventies they continued with the grammar school title. E.g. Queen Elizabeth's Grammar School, Ashbourne, Derbyshire.

Entrance to these schools is open to anyone who fulfils the school's admission criteria, which will usually include living within the school's catchment area. No selection test is used to determine suitability. Please note there are now only a small number of comprehensive schools in England with the name "Grammar" in their title.

Group 2 – These are independent fee paying secondary schools which in most cases went private when the comprehensives came in. E.g. Manchester Grammar School or Newcastle Royal Grammar School. Entrance will usually be via an entrance exam (either an 11+ or a 13+), as well as through a formal interview in some cases.

Group 3 – These are non-fee paying state schools which have remained as grammar schools, rather than change to comprehensive status. As such entrance is by a selection test known as the 11+ exam. E.g. Aylesbury Grammar School or Poole Grammar School.

However, not every one of this type of grammar school has the word "grammar" in their title. So they might be called "High School" or simply the name of their founder. E.g. Plymouth High School, or Sir Thomas Rich's School, Gloucestershire.

It is important therefore, when making your application for your child to sit the 11+ exam for a grammar school that you apply to the Group 3 type of grammar school.

How many of these grammar schools are there?

At the time of writing, there were 164 of these state grammar schools in England, with the possibility of a new one being opened in Sevenoaks, Kent. Entrance is through a child reaching a particular level in the 11+ exam, as well as fulfilling certain entry requirements as laid down in the school's admissions policy. For instance, that the child lives within the school's catchment/priority area, or is of a particular religious faith (if that grammar school is also a faith school).

You can read more about school admission policies in Chapter 4 on "Applying for the 11+".

As mentioned in Chapter 1, you will find traditional state grammar schools in these counties or metropolitan boroughs:- Berkshire, Bristol, Buckinghamshire, Cheshire, Cumbria, Devon, Dorset, Essex, Gloucestershire, Greater London, Greater Manchester, Kent, Lancashire, Lincolnshire, Liverpool, Middlesex, North Yorkshire, Redbridge, Shropshire, Staffordshire, Surrey, Warwickshire, West Midlands, West Yorkshire, Wiltshire, Wirral. The London boroughs which have grammar schools are: Barnet, Bexley, Bromley, Enfield, Kingston-upon-Thames, Redbridge and Sutton.

Please remember that just because a particular county has grammar schools, it doesn't always follow that there is a grammar school in every town. For example, in Lincolnshire there are grammar schools in the towns of Bourne, Grantham and Spalding, but not in the city of Lincoln itself. So it pays to do your research as to where your nearest grammar schools are, especially if you are thinking of moving into an area where there is a grammar school.

Tip: There is a complete list of state grammar schools with direct links to each grammar school on the website of The National Grammar Schools Association at this link:-

www.ngsa.org.uk/schools.php

Is it just grammar schools that have the 11+ exam?

Many parents have asked me this question over the years. The simple answer is "no". Private schools also have a form of the 11+ test, which in some cases will be set by the school itself. They also have an entry stream for children at 13+ and this exam is known as the "Common Entrance".

Then there are several state comprehensive schools which have an 11+ type entrance exam for some of their intake. This is because they can become oversubscribed by children who live outside their catchment area. Whilst children who live inside the school's catchment area will automatically be given a place, those outside may have to compete for a limited number of places. They would argue that the fairest way of doing this is to do so through an exam which tests their ability. They are known as "Partially Selective Schools" from their admissions policy of using a selection test for some of their intake. E.g. Edenham High School, Croydon.

Finally, there are "Bilateral Schools" which are not grammar schools, but comprehensives. However they do use an 11+ type selection test for some of their year 7 intake. This is because they have a "grammar stream" for brighter pupils and a non-selective stream for pupils who would be admitted anyway because they live in the school's catchment area. There are just eight of these bilateral schools in England and they are all in areas where there are grammar schools. E.g. St Bernard's High School for Girls, Southend-on-Sea.

Why are some grammar schools also known as "Academies"?

This isn't quite true, as the word "Academy" when applied to schools can mean three different things.
Firstly, "Academy" is the name given to many Scottish comprehensive schools which have been in existence since the 1970's. E.g. Ardrossan Academy, or Perth Academy.
Secondly, there are some former English Comprehensive schools which have the name Academy in their title. These are known as "Sponsored Academies" and were introduced during the last Labour Government to deal with failing schools to try and improve standards. E.g. Mossbourne Community Academy, Hackney.
Thirdly there are state Grammar schools with Academy Status. This means they are independent of the Local Authority and receive their funding direct from the government. They are sometimes known as "Converter Academies". At the time of writing the majority of the hundred and sixty four grammar schools in England had converted to Academy status. Many grammar schools now use the word, "academy" in their school title, which is where the confusion comes from.

What is it that makes grammar schools so popular with parents?

Many parents are attracted to grammar schools as the preferred type of school for educating their children. Why is this so?
The main ethos of the grammar schools seems to be their emphasis on academic excellence. All grammar schools have a sixth form and as such are geared into getting as many of their students into university or further education as possible. Many parents like these high academic ideals, which other types of secondary schools do not have in their opinion.

Also, many parents like the tradition of grammar schools, from the fact that many grammar schools have been in existence for hundreds of years, through to the age of their buildings, which give the grammar schools a certain character. Some parents also like the emphasis on greater discipline that grammar schools have over other types of schools. This can be seen in such rules as having their children called by their surname, or through showing respect to other pupils, or wearing their uniform in a presentable manner.

Finally, parents are attracted to the number of extra-curricular activities that grammar schools have, whether it be sports, musical activities or drama. Alongside these, are a wide range of clubs and societies such as debating, orienteering and chess, for example.

So all in all, it is hardly surprising that all grammar schools are over subscribed, as they are seen by many parents as the best type of secondary school there is. Also the fact that unlike private schools, there are no fees to be paid, is surely another attraction.

Why are some grammar schools known as "Super Selectives"?

The term "Super Selective" is one that has come into 11+ language in recent years by parents who compare one grammar school's "pass mark" with that of another. The more over subscribed a grammar school is, the harder it is to get in, due to the fact that its "pass mark" will be higher than other grammar schools in the same county. An example of this might be the score needed for guaranteed entry to Grammar School A was 336. Whilst for Grammar School B (also in the same county) the minimum score needed was 316. So it was much harder to get into Grammar School A and so this would be called a "Super Selective" grammar school by many parents, merely because it is more selective than Grammar School B. It does not necessarily mean that Grammar School A has better results at GCSE or A-Level than Grammar school B, just that it is more selective. Another factor in calling a grammar school, "Super Selective" is the fact that they may have two 11+ exam days. This is because they are so oversubscribed that they have to do a "sifting out" process so to speak. So a child might have to take a Part 1 11+ exam. Then if s/he gains a high enough mark in Part 1, they will be invited back to take the Part 2 11+ exam. Please note that this two part 11+ exam is only administered by a small number of grammar schools. Always check with each individual grammar school you are interested in to see if this is the case. The thing to remember is that there is no minimum score which is the same for every grammar school in the country, so some grammars will inevitably have a higher minimum score than others. It doesn't mean that one grammar school is better than another, just that its entry mark is different.

Before I go on to talk about how to apply for a place at a grammar school and other schools for that matter, I will briefly look at the other alternatives to grammar schools in the next chapter.

CHAPTER 3 – CHOOSING THE BEST SECONDARY SCHOOL FOR YOUR CHILD

Before deciding to apply for your child to sit the 11+, it is important to do some research about the possible choice of secondary schools in your area.

Researching your child's secondary school choices

It is vitally important that before you decide to put your child in for the 11+ exam, you thoroughly research **all** the secondary options open to your child. You should of course be given information from your local authority on all possible choices. They will send out information packs about the application process whilst your child is in Year 5. These are distributed through your child's primary or prep school. However, this may not arrive until a few months before the deadline date for applications. Many parents start to think about their child's secondary education at least a year earlier than the 11+ test, or even earlier than that. So the earlier you start in your research, the clearer in your mind you will be about your choices.

How do you get information on your local secondary schools?

There are several options here for parents to find out about their local secondary schools. The most obvious one is to look up each school on the internet. All secondary schools should have a school website which will tell you all about the school, such as its history, its successes, its admissions policy and its latest Ofsted report. This should give you as a parent a clearer picture of what each school is like and whether your child might be happy to go there. Always check to see whether the school is single-sex or co-educational, as this isn't always clear in the school name.

Apart from looking up each school's official website, it is worth putting the name of the school on an internet search engine and see what else comes up. You never know what you might find! At least it will give you a different perspective on the school from the often sanitised school websites. There will also be an entry for most secondary schools on the internet information website, Wikipedia, which should give you information on the school from a neutral point of view.

Secondary schools also produce a glossy prospectus in many cases, which again will give you plenty of information on the school. Those who are environmentally aware, will also produce an online downloadable version.

You can also find information on all the secondary schools in your area by logging onto your local authority website. If you are not sure what its name is or how to find it on the internet, you can log on to: www.local.direct.gov.uk and put in your postcode or town. This should take you to your local council/authority website and onto the education section, where you should be able to access all the information you need.

Tip: It is also worth keeping your eye on the pages of your local newspapers, as quite often schools are featured in the news section. Secondary schools keen on self promotion will from time feature in your local newspaper. It might be an article about a charitable action some pupils have done, or a sport's success, but at least it raises the school's profile in the minds of the general public.

The question of finding out about secondary schools from what other people say, be they neighbour, friend or acquaintance, is of course one that many parents use. This can be a two edged sword, as you are quite likely to hear something good about a particular school from one parent and then something bad about the same school from a different parent! If you do know someone whose son or daughter attends a secondary school, you could ask them about their views on their child's secondary school. It might encourage you or it might put you off. The important thing is to make up your own mind about the school from the different sources mentioned above and not just on the opinion of someone else.

Tip: There are several education based web forums on the internet which can be a hive of information for parents wanting more information about a particular school, as well as information on the 11+. You can register to join one or more of them and then ask a particular question. Be warned that the views discussed are those of individual parents and they may not be the majority view. Also there are certain "code words" and abbreviations used. Here are a few of them;- DC = Darling Child, DD = Darling Daughter and DS = Darling Son. For links to these forums, please see the chapter on 11+ Links at the end of this book.

There is another way of finding out more about your local secondary schools and that is to visit them yourself and look round them.

Secondary school open days

All secondary schools hold an open day (or evening) for potential pupils at least once a year. For grammar schools, these are usually in the summer term so that prospective pupils and their parents can see inside the school before the 11+ entrance exam takes place. For comprehensives (and some grammar schools) they are usually at the start of the autumn term in September or October. This is a good opportunity for both parents and their children to get a "feel" for each secondary school that they visit. Most open "days" actually occur in the evening on a week day after school. A few do take place on a Saturday, but these are in the minority.

Whilst there, you will be able to see most classrooms, along with exercise books - hopefully with work marked up to date!, display work and perhaps a practical display such as a Science experiment taking place. There will also be a speech/talk by the head teacher all about the school. This should include some information on the history of the school; mention of the school's recent results in GCSE and/or A Level; plus the special selling points of the school, such as achievements in Sport/Art/Music/Drama and so on. The head may well have a question and answer session afterwards, but this doesn't happen in every school. By the way, these talks by head teachers are not compulsory, so if tine is short, or long speeches are not your scene, you can skip this part of the evening.

The important thing for you as a parent is to learn as much about the school as possible. Many of the teachers, plus some pupils will be on hand to answer your questions, so don't be afraid to ask any questions you may have.

Here are some suggested questions:-

What is it like here?

How much homework do you get?

Is there any bullying?

What do you get a detention for? How long do they last?

What's the best/worst thing you like/dislike about the school?

Are there any rules you don't like?

There are plenty of other questions you might like to ask. There is no harm in taking a sheet of paper with you with the questions on it, so you don't forget to ask them!

Tip: You could go to an open evening and visit any of the secondary schools that you are interested in a year early. i.e. when your child is in Year 4. This could be either with your child or by yourself. Some parents do this as they feel it gives them a clearer vision of what they and their child will be aiming for in the 11+. Plus it can get quite busy at the end of the summer term prior to the 11+ with events at your child's primary school, as well as the secondary open evenings taking place. So if you have already been to visit the grammar schools a year early, that might save you some valuable time.

Other ways in which you can visit a secondary school

Not every parent can make it to a school open evening, so here are some alternatives to seeing round a school. The most obvious is to make an appointment as a prospective parent who would like to see the school. The advantage of this is that in most cases you will be shown round the school when it is "in session", i.e. the pupils are present. This will give you a chance to see the school as it really is, especially if you are there when the bell goes for a lesson change or break time. You can see how the pupils interact with each other and with adults they may pass. The disadvantage is that as school is in session you might not be allowed into the classrooms to see what the work is like, so as not to disturb the lesson. You can of course ask the same questions listed above if you are shown round by a pupil, but usually it will be a senior member of staff who shows you round.

Tip: Don't forget that many secondary schools do open their doors to the general public or to parents and their friends on other occasions. These might be when the Parent's Association holds a fund raising event such as a boot or table sale, or a cheese and wine tasting evening for example. Then there might be a football or hockey match which you could go and watch. Or there might be a concert or play held in the school hall which is open to the members of the public. Whilst these events will not give you as much access to the school as an open day would, you can at least observe some aspects of school life that you wouldn't normally see. Check the school's website to see if any of these sorts of events are taking place which you can go to.

Factors which might influence your choice of Secondary School

There are several factors which you should consider when making the choice of which Secondary School you would like your child to attend. Here are the main ones:-

1) Academic results. Many parents tend to go for the schools which perform the best in exams, be they GCSEs or A-Levels. You can get the latest figures for a school by looking on their website. Coupled with this is their position in the league tables. These can be found on the Government Education website at:

www.education.gov.uk/schools/performance

The website doesn't just show academic results, but also Ofsted results, absentee figures and "pupil characteristic data" which includes things like number of pupils on the role, pupils with Special Education Needs and pupils eligible for free school meals and the Pupil Premium.

Tip: When looking at league tables don't just look at how a school compares nationally, but find out how it compares with other schools in your local area. This will give you a truer picture of what it is like. An alternative website to the Government league tables site is this independent one which allows parents to compare schools in their local area based on the pupils' best GCSE results:-

www.schoolperformancetables.org.uk

2) The particular ethos of the school. This might be a faith school which follows a particular religion. If you follow that religion, this will be an important factor in choosing that school. Alternatively, the school may specialise in a particular subject that your child takes a keen interest in, such as Science, Maths, Languages, Drama, Music or Sport. This could also have a bearing on your choice of secondary school.

3) Distance from your home. This is important for many parents. Some prefer to be as near to their child's secondary school as possible. Other parents feel that although the school is quite a way from their home, it is worth making the sacrifice of a longer school day for the rewards offered.

Tip: Many grammar schools do provide buses for children who live outside the school's catchment area if there is enough demand. Check the school's website to see what they offer. Remember though that it will be harder to get into a school if you live a long distance away from it.

4) You know someone who already attends that school. This might be a neighbour's child, a relative, or even an older brother or sister. If they seem happy at that school, it might influence your choice of secondary school. Also, if you already have one child at a school, it will give your next child an advantage in the admissions criteria of that school. See the next section for more details on school admissions criteria.

Understanding School Admissions Policies

On each school website there should be a button at the top labelled "Admissions". If this doesn't seem to be there, it might well be hidden under another heading such as "School" or "other information". By law all schools, whether they be primary or secondary, should have an admissions policy in place. It is important that before you choose to apply for a place at that school that you read this information thoroughly

Most school policies include the following points:-

1) The order in which they allocate places for children entering the school in Year 7.

For grammar schools this will include information on the 11+ selection tests that they hold, such as when they take place and how many places will be available. In some cases they may state what the "cut off" score will be for successful candidates. In many cases, whether grammar or comprehensive, priority is often given to those who have an elder brother or sister already attending that school.

2) What the school's catchment or priority area is – if they have one.

This means that priority will be given to children who live within a designated area decided by the school. It might be a particular parish district or postcode of a town, or a given radius with the school at the centre. It might include "feeder schools" as well. i.e. those local primary schools which are within the school's catchment area. Some schools might actually have a set distance in miles, such as ten or twenty miles, as their catchment or priority area. This can be confusing as some schools define the distance "as the crow flies" (i.e. a straight line) on an ordnance survey map. Others might define the distance as a certain number of miles going along specified roads, as opposed to a straight line. If you live on the borders of this boundary line it is important that you discuss this with the school before you apply, to be doubly sure that you reside in the school's catchment/priority area. You can still apply for a school if you outside this area, though the mark needed for entry will be much higher than for those who live inside the designated area.

A word of warning. Over the years I have come across some quite desperate measures made by parents saying they live within a catchment area, when clearly they don't. These include giving the address of a divorced partner, or a grandparent, or even a close friend. Some have even gone to the extreme of renting out a house in the catchment area for six months or a year to prove they reside in a particular school's catchment area. Not only is this illegal, but both secondary schools and the local authority employ specially trained staff to check on any parent that they suspect of this type of fraud. Many secondary schools now insist on two or three proofs of address, such as original copies of your utility bill or council tax bill when you apply. Plus, they can always check with the child's primary school to see that the address given to them is the same for both schools.

3) Whether the school follows a particular faith or religion, in the case of faith schools. E.g. the school may follow the Roman Catholic faith or the Muslim religion.

The school may well ask for a reference from a priest or Imam to check that you are adherents to that religion. They may also ask for proof in the form of baptismal or confirmation certificates. I have heard of parents starting to go to church a few months before the date of a selection test, or even getting their child baptised in the hope of gaining a place at this type of selective state school. Again this is not to be encouraged and may well be noticed by the school.

4) Children who are in care or who have special educational needs.

Two important criteria that all schools have to have in their admissions policy is that priority will be given to certain types of children. One of these is for children who are in care or being "looked after" by the local authority. The other is children with a special educational needs statement which states that the child should attend a particular school. In practise this means that if a child has his or her name down as being suitable to attend a grammar school, that grammar school is obliged to offer a place to that child above all other applicants, provided they have reached the designated score in the 11+ exam.

Things to consider about grammar schools

When it comes to considering sending your child to a grammar school, there are certain points you should be aware of. The most obvious one is to check whether it is just for boys or girls, or co-educational? Also, is it a faith school? ie Catholic/Church of England. What about the school's admission policy? Does my child fit the criteria? Do I live in the catchment area? How easy is the journey to and from the school? Does it specialise in certain subjects that my child is interested in? How traditional is it? Are you aware of its rules and punishments and how strict it is? How much homework is set each day? Do I see my child as staying there on into the sixth form? Or might they leave after taking GCSE's?

These are all things that you need to consider and discuss with your child before deciding whether you should go ahead and apply for the 11+.

However the biggest question of all is this one......

Is my child suited to a grammar school education?

Within this question are several smaller questions. The most important of these is "Is my children bright enough to not only pass the 11+ exam, but also to cope with the work in a grammar school?" If you consider the fact that the majority of children, who take the 11+ exam, are not successful in gaining a place, then it would seem that many parents seem to think their children are brighter than they are.

How can you decide if your child is bright enough to gain a place at a grammar school?

The first thing you should consider is what your child's progress at school has been like over the past few years. For instance what are his/her reports like? Do they show consistent high marks and continued progress? What sets are they in for English and Maths? What do your child's class teacher and head teacher think?

Most grammar schools would expect those who pass their 11+ entrance exam to be at Level 5 in the National Curriculum when they leave primary school. The National average for all Year 6 leavers is Level 4. So ask yourself, "Is my child in Year 5 working towards level 4/5 in English and Maths for the National Curriculum? If so, then he/she perhaps should be a suitable candidate to take the 11+.

Your child should also have a reading age above their chronological age. So if a child in Year 5 who is aged ten, has a reading age of an 11 year old (or greater), then again this would indicate that she/he may a good candidate for taking the 11+. Combined with a high reading age, would be an interest in reading both fiction and non-fiction books, If your child is not an avid reader, but still intelligent, don't despair. There are other indicators of children being bright enough to cope with the 11+.

These might be on the writing side of things. Is his/her creative writing showing plenty of imagination, with a wide range of language? Plus is s/he fine with grammar, spelling and punctuation? Many schools use the writing side of the English 11+ exam as a way of deciding between two candidates who might have got the same scores on the other papers. So having good writing skills can be to your child's advantage in the 11+ exam.

One other area that might indicate suitability to succeed in the 11+ exam is your child's understanding of Mathematics. A basic benchmark would be knowing the times tables, both forwards and backwards. By that I mean that a child who knows his/her times tables would also be able to tell you what 56 divided by 8 is, or how many 12's there are in 132. Being quick on mental maths is also important. So if your child struggles with working out mathematical problems in their head, they may well struggle with the 11+ Maths paper, if that is set by the grammar school.

Another indicator of suitability to take the 11+ would be a child who shows an interest in problem solving and the challenge of finding a solution to a problem. Do they give up easily when faced with a challenge? Or do they persevere until a solution has been found?

Finally, a child who is able to think for themselves (at least most of the time!), and who is able to work quickly and confidently under pressure, should be able to cope with the demands of the 11+ exam. If they are self motivated, prepared to work hard and show an enthusiasm in going to grammar school, then you should let them go ahead and take the 11+ exam.

On the non-academic side, children who enjoy doing extra curricular interests, such as a sport, or some aspect of music or drama, usually go on to thrive in a grammar school environment. After all there is more to grammar school life than books and learning.

The most important thing for you to consider is whether your child shares your enthusiasm to go to a grammar school or not? It is no good deciding that your child is bright enough to take the 11+ exam and then finding that they haven't the slightest interest in going there. This needs to be a two-way process, with you as a parent starting the ball rolling at least at the beginning of year 5, or maybe earlier if you think your child is not that motivated to go to a grammar school.

Tip: If you are still unsure whether your child is good enough to take the 11+, you could pay for an educational psychologist to check your child's IQ (Intelligence Quotient). This will help you to see where they are in terms of the rest of their age group. Ideally a child with an IQ of around 130 would be a suitable candidate for taking the 11+ exam.

What about divorced/separated parents?

One situation that crops up from time to time is that of parents who are divorced or separated. What happens if one parent is for their child taking the 11+ and the other one isn't? Who decides? Does the parent who has custody of the child have the final say? Or do you let the child decide regardless of what the parents decide? This is one question which I can't answer for you. However, one way forward might be the two of you going together to see your child's head teacher to discuss the options. Or you could see someone from the local authority who could also act as an advisor in this situation. What matters above all is that your child is relaxed and happy about taking the 11+ and **does** want to go to a grammar school. If they aren't sure, maybe you need to look at other options.

Always look at non-grammar schools

No matter how sure you feel that your child is going to be successful in the 11+ and get into a grammar school, you should always consider the possibility that this may not happen. I have known several parents over the years who have been convinced that their child was going to pass the 11+ and so didn't put any alternative non-grammar school choices on their Local Authority application form. Then when their child didn't pass for whatever reason, they were at a loss as to what to do next.

It is not only sensible to have an alternative plan ready, should this possibility happen, but also common sense. So what options should you look at?

Your local comprehensive school

The first and most obvious thing is to consider taking up a place at your local comprehensive school. You may even have a choice of several comprehensives which will be offered to you, so you could consider all of them, as long as they are within reasonable travelling distance. When it comes to filling in the local authority application form, it is advisable to include at least one of your local comprehensives on the list after the grammar school(s) you have included. (See the next chapter for more details).

Again, I have known parents who haven't bothered going to the open evening at their local comprehensive(s) prior to the 11+. Then once their child was not successful in getting into a grammar school, and they were offered a place at the comprehensive, they wished they had gone! It is quite likely that many of your child's school friends may well be going to the local comprehensive. So your own child going there will mean s/he will be among his or her peers, which might not always be the case with a grammar school.

Also in the long term, many parents of children who don't get into a grammar have to admit that it is better to be at the top end of the class in a comprehensive, than struggling near the bottom of the class at a grammar.

If you are still 100% anti your child going to the local comprehensive, there are several other options to consider. The first is going to a private school.

What about private schools?

You may have dismissed the private school option merely because you know you cannot afford the fees, which can range from between £2,000 to £5,000 a term. However, there are some alternatives to this. Virtually all private schools offer some form of bursary, scholarship or assisted place scheme, where the school will pay some or all of the fees for a child who is particularly strong or gifted in one area. In most cases it will be for music or sports, so if you feel that your child is gifted in these areas, this could be an option you could pursue. It is worth looking at the websites of private schools in your locality if you are thinking of doing this.

Virtually all private schools have their own version of the 11+ as a way of checking the child's suitability for their school. Therefore your child would have to take the school's entrance exam to gain a place. This may well be several months after the 11+ has taken place, usually in the months of January to March, but check with the school for precise dates. From my experience, the standard of most private school entrance exams is usually easier than that of the 11+. So your child may well pass this exam, even if they weren't successful in the 11+. It is worth bearing in mind though that many private schools do include a formal interview with each child as part of the selection process. If your child is likely to get particularly nervous or tongue-tied in a situation like this, then maybe this might not be an option for you.

Finally, I have known some parents who were so desperate for their child not to attend their local comprehensive, that they somehow managed to find the funds to pay for a private education for their child. This may have been through re-mortgaging their home, or through a bank loan, or through cashing in a savings plan. It is surprising when push comes to shove, the things people will do to achieve something they want so much!

Free schools

If you live in a town where there is a free school, this could be an option for you to consider. At the time of writing there were approximately two hundred and fifty Free Schools in England, the first opening in 2011. Not all are secondary though; some are primary, some are special schools and some cater for children right through from the ages of 5 to 16. The main difference to other state schools is that they receive their funding direct from the government and not the local authority. As such they are not obliged to follow the National Curriculum and so can choose which subjects to teach, or not to teach. Plus at the moment, the teachers do not have to have the Qualified Teaching Status qualification.

Many of the Free Schools are run by charitable trusts including different religious groups. So one free school might be Jewish; another Muslim, and another Church of England. At the moment Free Schools which are based on a particular religion are obliged to allow no more than 50% of their intake from their own faith group, if they become over subscribed. They can also dictate the times of the school day and the dates of their terms.

Of course there are plenty of arguments for and against Free Schools, but they do seem to be popular with parents. More Free Schools are opening all the time, so it looks like they are a phenomenon that is here to stay. As to their future success, only time will time.

For more information on Free Schools see the links section at the back of this book.

Home schooling

The final option which some parents consider, is that of teaching their children at home, which is also called "Elective Home Education". Some parents, whose child missed out on a place at grammar school by just a few points, decide to go on the school's waiting list in the hope that a place will eventually turn up. They choose home schooling as the best way forward, rather than sending their child to another secondary school. Whether they follow this option for a few months or even years depends on how much of a success they can make it. Please be aware that many local authorities take a dim view of this practice and so it would be prudent to check with them if they are happy with this arrangement.

Whilst it is perfectly legal to educate your child at home, you do need to let your local education authority know, as well as the secondary school that your child was offered a place at. Also you don't have to follow the National Curriculum if you choose not to do so. You do not get any funding to do this, so you need to think carefully before you undertake such an option. If you have enough money, you can pay for a private tutor to come to your house to teach your child either part-time or full-time.

Of course, home schooling will mean a huge commitment on the side of the parent, as well as the need for the child to "knuckle down" with their work. Also children who are taught at home will miss out on many social aspects of being in a school with their contemporaries.

For more information on home schooling, see the links section at the back of this book.

In the next chapter I will look at the complicated subject of applying for a place at a grammar school as well as your local authority non-grammar schools.

CHAPTER 4 – THE APPLICATION PROCESS FOR GRAMMAR AND OTHER SECONDARY SCHOOLS

In this chapter we will be looking at how to apply for the 11+ as well as for secondary schools in general.

There are two parts to the application process

Once you and your son/daughter have decided that sitting the 11+ is the best way forward, then you have to start the ball rolling with the 11+ application process.

It is important for you to be aware that there are two separate parts in the application process for secondary schools. The first part is applying to take the 11+ exam at the grammar school(s) that you would like your child to attend. The second part is to fill in the local authority application form, where you put down your choices of secondary schools (including grammar schools) for your child to attend after they leave primary school. This is done once you have received the results of the 11+ test. I will now go into more detail about both these parts of the application process.

Let's start with the 11+ part first.

The 11 Plus application process

Since the New Schools Admission Code came into force in 2012, all grammar schools have had to change the date on which the 11+ exams take place. Originally most grammar schools had their tests sometime in the spring term, with results being given out at the beginning of the summer term. Now the 11+ exam dates have been moved forward in the school year to September and October, in almost every case. This is so that grammar schools can notify parents of whether their son or daughter has reached the required mark in the 11+, before the parents fill in the Local Authority application form, which has to be in by 31st October. This cut off date gives the local authorities enough time to process the thousands of applications from parents, who need to be notified of their child's secondary school by National Results Day (or National Offer Day, or National Allocation Day) on 1st March.

In practice, this means is that there is less time to prepare for the 11+ than in the past, and also less time to make up your mind as to which school(s) you wish to send your child to.

As mentioned earlier, there is plenty of information on the internet about the various secondary schools in your area. The actual details about applying for a place at a grammar school will be on that school's website as well as in their prospectus. Also details will be available at the open evenings/days they hold in the summer term. However, it is your local education authority that will contact you sometime in the summer term with details of the procedure for applying for a place at secondary schools in your area. Usually this contact will be in the form of a folder in an A4 envelope (containing the forms and information), which your child will be given at their primary school or prep school. If you are getting worried about not getting this folder, you can always check with your child's school or the local Education Authority as to when these packs are sent out. The information in the packs should also be on the Local Authority website under "Secondary Admissions" or something similar.

The important thing at this stage is to make up your mind which grammar school(s) you are going to apply to. Once you have made up your mind, you will need to get hold of the grammar school application form(s) to fill in and send back. This application form has different names depending on the area, such as SIF Supplementary Information Form (SIF) in Essex or the Optional Test Form (OTF) in Birmingham. If you don't fill this in and send it back, either by post or by e-mail by the deadline, your child will not be able to sit the 11+ exam and so go onto a grammar school. These forms are usually ready for parents to receive by post or download from the internet from April/May onwards. The closing date varies from school to school - some being as early as May and some as late as September, so there may or may not be plenty of time to make your choice(s). Most will ask you for one or two proofs of address, as well as for a current photo of your child to be signed by your child's current head teacher in many cases. So make sure that you have these to hand when you apply.

If the grammar school you wish you child to apply to is in another area from which you live, you will still have to fill in an application form for that grammar school. In this case it would be advisable to contact the grammar school directly to check on your child's suitability as shown on their admissions policy, as well as asking for them to send you an application form. In fact it doesn't matter where you live in the country, you can still apply for a place at any grammar school in England if you wish. Don't forget that the further that you live away from that school, the higher the score needed to gain entry will be. Plus there may well be a clash of dates for when each grammar school has its 11+ test day.

In areas or towns where there is more than one grammar school for you to apply to, you will have to fill out separate application forms for each grammar school, unless a consortium exists in that area. (see below for information on Consortium Grammar Schools). It is a good idea to double check the dates (and times) on which each grammar school will be holding their 11+ exam, just in case the dates clash. If this is the case, you may be able to sit one of the 11+ tests on an alternative date, as most grammar schools do have an alternative date for children who can't take the exam on a particular day, such as on a Saturday for religious reasons.

Some areas have overcome this problem by grouping the grammar schools together in one area in a group known as a "Consortium". This means that you can apply for more than one grammar school in a particular area, but only have to sit the 11+ exam once. Details about where consortiums operate now follow.

What is a grammar school consortium?

In some areas several local grammar schools have joined together for ease of administration of the 11+ exam to the advantage of both the schools and the parents. This group of grammar schools (and in some cases selective comprehensives) is known as a consortium.

At present there are six consortiums for grammar and other selective schools in the following areas. These are:

The Birmingham Consortium, which includes schools in Aston, Camp Hill, Five Ways, Handsworth and Sutton Coalfield.

The Essex Consortium, which includes schools in Chelmsford, Colchester and Southend-on-Sea.

The Lincolnshire Consortium of Grammar Schools which includes schools in Grantham, Skegness, Sleaford and Spalding.

The Shropshire, Walsall and Wolverhampton Consortium of Grammar Schools which includes schools in Newport (Shropshire), Walsall and Wolverhampton.

The Slough Consortium of Grammar Schools which includes schools in Langley, Slough and Upton.

The South-West Hertfordshire Consortium of Schools, which includes schools in Bushey, Chorleywood, Rickmansworth and Watford.

There is also a North London Consortium for private schools holding an 11+ type test in the areas of North and Central London. (Please note these are all girls' schools).

See the 11+ Links chapter at the end of this book for links to the consortium websites.

Tip: If you are applying to sit the 11+ exam via a consortium you may be given a choice of which school to sit the exam at. This means that you don't necessarily have to take the exam at the school that is your first choice, which maybe oversubscribed and busy on the 11+ exam day. Some parents choose a less popular school as the venue for their child's 11+ test, which may be quieter and thus less stressful.

Opting in or opting out?

It is also worth remembering that in some areas all year 6 children in state schools take the 11+, unless their parents say they do not want them to take the 11+. This is known as "opting out" and only takes place in one or two areas, such as Buckinghamshire. The other grammar school areas rely on the parents to make the application. So please be aware of this.

Make sure you get a reply to your 11+ application

Once you have sent in your grammar school application form(s), you should get a letter or e-mail of confirmation from the grammar school a few days later. If you haven't received this after a week or so you should contact the school to let them know. The reply you get will give you details of the venue where your child will sit the 11+ exam, as well as times and entrances you should go to on the day of the 11+ test. Your child will also be given a candidate number for the test. You might also get information on where you can wait in the school - if the grammar school caters for this. Otherwise you will have to drop your son/daughter off at the school and return at the end of the session to pick them up.

Special Needs and applying for the 11+

If your child has a special educational need or a health issue such as dyslexia or autism, the grammar school should be notified of this at the time of application. Usually they have a separate form for you to put in the details. Always check with the grammar school concerned about this if it doesn't say on their website. You may well have to supply supporting documentation from a health professional such as a doctor or consultant,

Applying from abroad for grammar schools

It is possible to take the 11+ if you live abroad, **provided** the grammar school gives the go ahead for this to take place and you are a UK citizen. They may well need evidence from you that you will be moving back to the UK and have a job/home in the catchment area. If you are in this situation, I would advise you to contact the grammar school and the local education office as soon as possible in advance of the exam for advice. Your child's current school outside the UK should also be informed, as that is the place where your child will be likely to sit the exam. I have heard in some cases of children living abroad, flying in to the UK to take the exam at a grammar school. This is an exception, rather than a rule and again you would need to check with the grammar school concerned about this.

Grammar schools that accept boarders

An alternative for British Citizens living abroad, that can't move back to the UK because of their work, is to consider grammar schools that accept boarders. There are a handful of grammar schools that do this and your first port of call would be the State Boarding School's Association who have more information about this on their website:-

http://www.sbsa.org.uk/

Applying to take the 11+ exam a year early

In very exceptional circumstances some children do take the 11+ a year early. These are super bright children, who may be several years ahead of their contemporaries academically. It is felt that they would be better off in a grammar school, doing more advanced work than they would in year 6 at their primary school. If you feel that your child fits into this category, you would need to speak to your child's current head teacher, as well as the head of the grammar school you hope they will attend. If they were not successful taking the 11+ a year early, they would probably not be able to take it the following year, unless the head teacher was agreeable.

Tip: The National Association for Gifted Children may be able to give you advice on this. Their website address is: www.nagc.org

Getting the 11+ results

Once the 11+ exam has been taken, there will be a nerve wracking few weeks as you wait for the results of the test. You will either receive a letter in the post, or an e-mail, informing you of your child's score and where they have come on the list of the whole "cohort" of children who have taken the test. It won't actually say whether your child has passed the exam or not, nor will it say that the grammar school is offering you a place. Instead it will give you details of the acceptable scores suitable for gaining entry to the grammar school. In other words the grammar schools now can only say "between the lines" that your child has gained a high enough score (or not) to be accepted into their school. This means that you can now go on to apply for a place at the grammar school (using the local authority application form) based on your child gaining a high enough score to guarantee entry.

Usually the grammar schools or consortiums have a guidance sheet, which will help you make up your mind whether it is worth applying for a place at the grammar school or not. For example, the Essex Consortium has used a "traffic light" system in the past to indicate which scores are good enough to reach entry into each particular grammar school. So green indicates that the child's score is good enough to gain a place at the grammar school, whilst orange/amber would indicate they may be offered a place if their mark was above the minimum score. Even if the score was a few marks down on this minimum mark, it still might be worth applying. With red, it would indicate that their score was not good enough to apply for a place.

So your child has sat the 11+ exam and has reached the minimum bench mark for the grammar school. What happens next?

The local authority application form

Since 2012, a new application form has been in use for every year 6 child, which is sent out from your local authority. To confuse things it has several different names depending on which area you live in. The various names I have come across include: the Local Authority Application Form (LAAF), the Local Authority Preference Form (LAPF), the Common Application Form (CAF), the Common Entry Form (CEF), or the Single Application Form (SAF). So be aware of what the form is called in your particular area.

This is an application form that all parents **have** to fill in, whether they are expecting to send their child to a grammar school or not. This is the form where parents put down their order of choice for which secondary school they wish their child to attend from Year 7 onwards. This may or may not include a grammar school in their choice.

Here are some things you should be aware of when filling in your form. If you are applying for a grammar school, you should always put down **all** the grammar schools you wish your child to attend **first**, provided they have reached the minimum score for acceptance. (See next section for "borderline scores") Then put down other schools that you would like your child to go to - if they are not successful in gaining a place at your first choice grammar school(s). You should get a minimum of three choices, though this may be five or six depending on the local authority. It is up to you as to how many choices you make, but it is always best to have at least one comprehensive that you are happy with on the form.

I have known some parents to put one grammar school first, then a comprehensive second and then another grammar school third. The local authorities always treat each choice as a separate entity and go down the list in numerical order. This is known as the Equal Preference System. So if your child was not offered a place at the first grammar school you put as your first choice, s/he would automatically go down to the second school on the list, which is the comprehensive, rather than to the second grammar school on the list. This means that if they scored a high enough mark to gain entrance to the second grammar school, but not the first, they would be offered a place at the comprehensive, as that is number two on their list.

Tip: Most Local Authorities now have certain members of staff trained to help parents with filling in the Local Authority application form. They can be useful if you are pulling your hair out, trying to make sense of the form, or when you are not sure which schools to put down in which order. So please ask your local authority if you do need help in filling out this application form. Some authorities even post guidance videos on line to help make the application process easier.

What happens if my child scored just above or below the cut off mark?

If your child was "borderline", i.e. gained a score either just above or just below the cut off mark, it is always worth putting that school as your number one choice. This is because not every child who reaches that cut off mark goes on to take up the grammar school place offered to them. They may go onto a private school, move away from the area, or just decide not to take up the place. It is always advisable to discuss this option with both your child's head teacher and the grammar school concerned, before making any final decision. You can also ask to be put on the school's waiting list, if your child's 11+ score was just below the cut off mark. As explained above, places do become available as the system works through the various applications.

Please note. This is not the time to appeal against the decision of the grammar school. You can only appeal once the formal placements have been made on or after 1st March. You can of course ask for your child's exam paper(s) to be remarked if you feel strongly that your child should have got a high enough mark in the 11+ test(s).

Applying for secondary schools by children with special needs

Usually, children with a statement of special educational needs do not apply for a secondary school place via the Local Authority application form. Instead they follow a different procedure. The child's SEN caseworker will know the procedure and would be the best person to advise you on this process.

Make sure you get the Local Authority application in on time

It is vitally important that you make sure that you send your child's secondary school application form in on time. The closing date is 31st October, wherever you live in England. As this date is usually in the Autumn Term half term holiday period, make sure that if you are away on holiday, you have remembered to send it off. In the past you usually sent it by post, but with the advent of the internet most authorities allow you to send it via the internet. You should get an acknowledgement that they have received the form as well, to put your mind at peace.

Most councils do allow late applications from my experience, but these will not be dealt with until all the others have been processed, which could jeopardise your application.

In the next chapter I will look at how you as a parent can help your son or daughter prepare for the 11+, so they will be able to face the exam with confidence.

CHAPTER 5 – PREPARING YOUR CHILD FOR THE 11+ EXAM

Should you as a parent be preparing your child for the 11+?

Many parents find preparing their child for the 11+ quite a daunting experience. They are not sure how to go about it; what practice papers to buy, what subjects are set, whether to have a tutor for their child or not, and whether to even bother.

Some parents believe that it is the job of their child's primary or prep school to do all the preparation. After all you are paying for this via your taxes or the school fees. Some believe (as do some heads of the grammars) that a child doesn't need any preparation at all and if they are bright enough, they will pass the 11+ exam with ease.

From my experience I would say that some form of preparation is absolutely essential for your child. After all, any student will revise for an exam that they are taking. Preparation is necessary to help pupils understand the types of questions they will have to face in the 11+, and to help build up their self-confidence in taking such a stressful exam. This exam is the most important test that they will have to face in their lives to date and if they go into the exam "cold", they can quite easily panic and "freeze" because the whole process is quite alien to them.

Apart from using the many and varied practice papers that are available on the market, there are plenty of things that you as a parent can teach your child at home in your everyday lives. If you encourage your child to think for themselves more, they will become adept at "thinking on their feet", or thinking logically, which is what so much of the 11+ exam requires of a child. The examiners are not just looking for a child who can answer the questions correctly, but one who is able to interpret logically the best way to find that answer.

Preparing for the 11+ from a young age

If you as a parent are reading this book with children who are still a few years off taking the 11+, there are plenty of things that you can be doing to encourage them in their learning. It goes without saying that a lot of this will help them generally with their education, but it will also lay the foundations for giving them the best start in preparing for the 11+.

The most important thing you can do is to encourage them in their reading habits. If you can instil a love of reading in your child from an early age you will have won half the battle! You can do this by reading to them each day, so that when they start reading themselves, you will have encouraged them to have an enjoyment of reading that they take with them into adulthood. If you can join your local library and borrow books from an early age, they will get into the habit of choosing books that they can take home and enjoy. If the libraries hold summer holiday reading clubs, encourage them to take part

Tip: I know many parents who have a notebook that they keep for their children to put in new words that they don't know the meaning of. Then they can look them up in a dictionary and hopefully remember both the meaning of the word and how to spell it. This can be done as soon as they start reading and is still a useful thing to do right up to the 11+.

The other important thing you as a parent can do to help your child is to encourage them with their mathematical skills. Right from an early age, help them to learn their times tables, right up to 12. Obviously they won't be able to learn them all in one go, but if they are competent with their times tables by the time they sit the 11+, this will be a good foundation for understanding the rest of the Maths concepts that they will learn in primary school.

It is also equally important that they have a good understanding of the functions of the four rules of number. That is how to add, subtract, multiply and divide in all the various ways. Most of this is what they should be learning at school, but if you as a parent can encourage them at home as well, this will hold them in good stead when it comes to getting ready for the 11+.

Tip: It is worthwhile investing in a wall chart that shows the times tables and other mathematical concepts, which can be put on the fridge or a wall somewhere in your house. Visual aids are great tools for helping your children to learn and remember important Maths concepts. You could also get one which has parts of speech and/or punctuation marks for the English side of things.

How soon should I be preparing my child for the 11+ exam?

Normally I would say a child should start his/her preparation about six to twelve months before the date of their actual 11+ test. Obviously a lot will depend on how confident and able your child is. I know of some parents who start paying out for a private tutor in year 4 (or even earlier!), in the hope that their child will be at an advantage over other children when it comes to 11+ day. Personally I would say, as long as you are supporting and encouraging your child in their school work and educating them in practical ways at home, then year 5 is the time to start you child's 11+ preparation. After all, most children at this age are still nine years old and need to "have a life" outside of school and the 11+.

Tip: Get yourself a diary or a wall calendar so you can keep a check on all the various dates that come up. These will include closing dates for both the 11+ application form(s) and the local authority application forms; the dates of the various schools' open days, plus dates of other 11+ related events, such as mock test days. Plus, your own holidays can also be recorded. If you are organised in this way it will take away a lot of the stress that the 11+ brings to a parent.

What should I be doing at home to help my child prepare for the 11+ exam?

Firstly, always encourage your child in his or her schoolwork. Most parents will already be doing this. For instance, asking your child what s/he has done at school each day, either academically or otherwise. Make sure that you check any work books that they bring home to see if there are any problem areas.

Also check that they are completing their homework on time and to a good standard. If there are any areas they are struggling in, don't be afraid to consult your child's teacher about these. You can always buy work books for Maths and English from either the internet or your local bookshop to "give them a boost" if you desire, or if your child's teacher recommends it. But don't force too much home work on them in the early part of year 5. Try and keep a work/play balance with your child all through this process.

It is also important that you encourage them to read at home - not just their reading book from school, but also a variety of different texts, such as newspapers, encyclopaedias (for research), magazines, comics, etc. (see below for more details).

Tip: You could try searching on the internet for "11+ reading lists" to see what other schools/teachers/tuition centres recommend as reading preparation for the 11+.

Secondly, keep in close contact with their class teacher to see if there are any areas of the 11+ subjects that they find difficult, especially in Maths and English. In Maths do they know all their times tables? What about the four rules? (adding, subtracting, multiplying and dividing) Are there any weaknesses in these areas? Are they competent with decimals, fractions, percentages, time, money and shape, etc? In English, how is their punctuation and grammar? Do they know their parts of speech? Do they understand things like homophones, prefixes and suffixes, contractions and synonyms/antonyms.

Finally, they can prepare for the 11+ exam by attempting 11+ practice papers. They not only help the child get used to the type of questions they will have to face in the 11+ exam, but also teach them to work quickly and efficiently under timed conditions. See next section for more details.

Tip: It might be a good idea to set learning goals or targets for your child to reach as they go through their 11+ preparation. This might be for example to learn the meanings of a set number of words each week, or to be competent at a different mathematical topic such as decimals or fractions. It is really up to you just what targets you set, but don't have too many as you child could be overwhelmed by all the pressure this could create. If s/he receives a lot of homework from school, bear in mind that too much work at home could be detrimental. So try and keep a balance between school homework and your own work if at all possible.

When should my child use 11+ practice papers?

Perhaps the answer to this question should be "only when your child is ready to use them". By that I mean many parents start using 11+ practice papers far too early, usually at the start of Year 5, or even in Year 4. The problem with this is that this is the time when most children are still learning many of the skills and knowledge needed for the 11+. Obviously if the 11+ exam they are taking involves Non-verbal and/or Verbal Reasoning it might be worth buying some "how to" books to get an understanding of what is required in these subjects. There is no harm in using practice papers at home, as long as they are used sparingly in the six months before the 11+ exam and not as a way of "cramming" your child in the last few weeks before the exam. They do help the child get used to the types of questions they have to answer in the 11+ exam, as well as helping them get used to working under timed conditions.

The problem I find time and again with some parents is that they think the more 11+ practice papers you do, the more likely their child will pass the 11+. I would say that it is not a question of *quantity*, but rather *quality*. i.e. how you use the practice papers. A wise parent will use 11+ practice papers as a way of getting their child used to the questions that are set in the 11+, as well as learning about how a child needs to time himself/herself under timed conditions. When your child gets a certain question type wrong, that is the time to sort out the problem, so that in future they will get that type of question correct. This does not mean doing every 11+ practice paper under the sun, but rather using them sparingly and effectively. Get your child to learn from his/her mistakes and be aware of how quickly they need to work at the paper. A "drip-feed" approach, as opposed to a "force-feed" approach will pay dividends in the end. The worst scenario I have come across, is one parent who made his child do three papers a day for months before the actual test. No wonder the poor child was not successful!

Tip: when buying 11+ practice papers, most parents just go to their high street bookshop and buy whatever is on the shelves. What they don't realise is that the big high street bookshops tend to just have about three or four different educational publishers' 11+ titles in stock. If you go onto the internet, you will find a much wider choice and variety of 11+ practice papers. In fact there are approximately thirty different publishers of 11+ practice papers on the Internet. Try keying in a variety of search words such as "11+ Verbal Reasoning" or "11+ publishers" for example and see what comes up.

Is it worth paying for a private tutor for my child?

This is a question which many parents agonise over, especially as it seems that all their classmates are being tutored. A lot will depend on your child's overall ability. Some children benefit from the one to one approach that a tutor brings, especially if you as a parent find it difficult teaching your own child at home. Other children do not need extra tuition if they are doing academically well at their primary/prep school. For more information on tutors see the next chapter, where I go into detail about all you need to know about tutors and tutoring.

Other practical ways you can help your child

Here are some other ways that you as a parent can help your child get ready for the 11+ exam. In fact, many of these tips are things you can do with any child to help them gain a practical understanding of both Mathematical and Language concepts that they come across in their everyday lives.

Vocabulary

It is vitally important in the 11+ that your child has a good all round vocabulary, so it goes without saying, the more reading they do, the better. It doesn't have to be just fiction books from school or your local library. There are plenty of other sources. For instance, newspapers, comics, football programmes, or non-fiction books on a topic they may be interested in.

Tip: Some 11+ tests in English quite often use the "classic" texts which have old fashioned English language in them. It might be worth getting one or two adapted versions of these sorts of books to get them used to the archaic language in them.

If your child is not that bothered with reading, you could try audio books to whet their appetite. Maybe put one on in the car when your travel somewhere; or even take your child to a bookshop to choose one they might like. Then buy them the book version to read at home as well. Apart from making sure your child learns his/her vocabulary for spelling tests at school, you could buy vocabulary books for them to practise spellings at home. Then there are puzzle books (for children) you can use which have a variety of crosswords, anagrams and word searches in them. These are very useful in building up their vocabulary and spelling knowledge.

Tip: Most schools recommend that your child has his/her own dictionary and thesaurus to use at home. If you haven't got these two tools, it is certainly worth getting them for your child, as they will help not only with spellings, but also with meanings and synonyms.

Writing

If you can encourage your child to practise writing, that will also help them considerably in the 11+. One way is to keep a diary. Not every child will want to do this, but if they received one as a birthday or Christmas present, it might spur them on to use it. Or if you are going away on holiday, you could get them to keep a journal of all the things they do and see whilst they are away. I know it is old fashioned, but letter writing is another form of writing that they could do. Perhaps writing thank you letters after a birthday or Christmas, or even sending postcards to their friends whilst they are on holiday?

Some children do enjoy creative story writing and if your son/daughter is one of these, it is worth encouraging them in this hobby. For instance, buy them blank books for them to write their stories in. Maybe get them to read out loud what they have written to an audience, such as younger brothers and sisters, or grandparents, so that they have something to aim for.

Finally if your child's handwriting is not that neat, it is important that they do practise handwriting exercises leading up to the 11+, as marks can easily be lost in the 11+ due to illegible handwriting.

Maths

Apart from doing Maths from workbooks and practice papers, it is always useful to do some practical Maths activities with your child from time to time. These might include the following:-

Working out the cost of different items of shopping when you go to the supermarket. E.g. How much would five of these cereals/tins/packets cost?

Working out how much the petrol costs when filling up your car at the petrol station.

Working out the total mileage or distance on a car journey.

Doing mental maths problems whilst sitting together at meal times.

E.g. what is seven times eight? What is six more than twenty-nine?

What is thirty two minus nineteen, with fourteen added on? (You can start off with easy examples and then move on to harder questions the nearer you get to the 11+).

Also the Japanese puzzle, Sudoku, is a good stimulus for your child to practise his/her Maths on. There are junior versions of this, which will be more suitable for your child, rather than the adult version.

The Maths questions on the Channel 4 TV quiz programme, *Countdown* are also good for practising mental maths. So too is the English words section for building up your child's vocabulary. The BBC 2 programme, *Beat the Brain* is another TV programme which is worth watching, not just for its Maths questions, but also for its English and Reasoning questions, all of which are great for preparing your child for the 11+. You could even watch these programmes as a family, thus encouraging your child to revise in a fun way.

Tip: Many episodes of these two TV programmes can be found on You Tube to watch if they are not currently on TV. Also, you could watch them at a time which suits you best.

Other things which can help your child

Some parents I know have put up maps of the world or Britain or flags of the world on their fridges or kitchen walls. Or they have a globe in the house. Whilst these are not necessarily a requirement for the 11+, they can be useful in building up your child's general knowledge.

Getting your child to make up quizzes which they can try out on their friends or siblings is another way to stimulate their learning and reading.

Puzzle books with word searches or crosswords in, are also worth using.

Card games are also useful in developing your child's mental maths. Also board games like Draughts, Chess, Scrabble, Monopoly, Mastermind, etc as well as jigsaws, if used from a young age, can be useful foundations for the 11+.

Don't be afraid to educate your children culturally too. Family days out don't have to be just to theme parks, but can also be to historical places like castles, stately homes, museums, parks and gardens. Organisations like the National Trust and English Heritage do cater for children much more than in the past, with various activities for children at their sites.

Finally, listen to your child and find out which things they like doing. If possible, when they need a break from their work, let them do that activity.

Your attitude to your child is very important

During the whole period leading up to the 11+, it is important that you as a parent maintain a positive attitude, both with your child and in private. It is very easy to pass on your worries and concerns to your son/daughter. It is crucial that you are there to support your child and not to criticise them. If they are finding it hard coping with both their 11+ preparation work, as well as their school work, don't be afraid to give them a break. Maintaining a balance between their school work and their 11+ work can be hard at times, so if you see your child wilting under all this work, it might be sensible to hold back with the 11+ work for a few days at least. The 11+ is not the be all and end all of a child's life when they are ten, so let them have a life outside of academic work as well.

Helping your child to relax

The key to your child being successful in the 11+ is not just concentrating on the 11+ preparation, but also doing some "11+ relaxation" from time to time. This can take various forms, which I shall now discuss.

I hear of parents who stop their children from doing other extra curricular activities such as ballet, football, swimming or drama club, in the lead up to the 11+. Personally I see no need to do this, especially if your child is particularly talented in these sorts of activities. They can be useful for "letting off steam", as well as giving your child a break from the stresses of 11+ preparation.

Also there is no harm in giving your child a treat every so often, such as a visit to the cinema, or a sporting event, or a day out at the weekend. A break from academic work at home does help your child to relax and so be more energised to work afterwards.

A positive mental attitude from you to your child is worth its weight in gold, rather than a constant nagging at them about the 11+. Be fair with your child. Let them watch their favourite TV programme, rather them making them do homework. The homework can be done once the programme has finished. Try and have a timetable in place, so there is time for relaxation each evening/weekend, as well as time for school work and time for 11+ work. Keeping the right balance between work and relaxation will pay dividends in the future.

To end this chapter, I have compiled a list of the top ten "mistakes" I have seen by parents over the years, regarding their attitudes to their children over the 11+. Hopefully, you as a parent will avoid making these mistakes with your child.

The top 10 mistakes made by parents towards their children over the 11+ exam

1) Making their children sit the 11+ exam when they haven't got the ability to pass.

2) Making their child do too many 11+ practice papers.

3) Threatening their children with a punishment if they do not do their 11+ work or do not pass the 11+.

4) Bribing them with a reward if they can pass the 11+ exam.

5) Stopping them from attending other after school activities or parties.

6) Pressurising their children by going on and on about the 11+.

7) Assuming that their child will pass the 11+ without doing any preparation.

8) Buying 11+ practice papers without checking to see if they are suitable preparation materials for the exam they are taking.

9) Believing the myths of other parents about the 11+ and grammar schools.

10) Leaving 11+ preparation until the last minute. i.e. just a few weeks or days before the exam.

In the next chapter, I will look at the much debated question about whether to have a tutor for you child or not, and what all this entails.

CHAPTER 6 – THE QUESTION OF TUTORING AND THE 11+

The whole question of having your child tutored or not, is one that all parents putting their child in for the 11+ exam have to face at sometime. Certainly there has been a phenomenal growth in the tutoring business within the past ten years, with individual tutors, tutoring agencies, tutoring websites and tutoring "schools" springing up in any area where the 11+ takes place. I have even heard of some primary schools employing a private tutor to tutor their 11+ pupils in after school groups.

Where do you start? Well there are three main tutoring paths that a parent can go down, apart from the option of not having a tutor at all.

Some parents do decide not to bother with a tutor, partly because of the cost and partly because they believe that the education that their child is receiving at their present school should be sufficient. This is the path that some grammar school heads would prefer you take, as they believe that tutoring for the 11+ can have a detrimental effect on a child's progress later on in grammar school. The thinking being, that if a child needs to be tutored to pass the 11+, then they clearly aren't good enough to pass under "their own steam" so to speak. So one or two years down the line they may struggle with the standard of work involved if they "just scraped in".

On the other hand there are some grammar schools that seem to encourage tuition (of sorts) by selling past 11+ tests on their school's website for parents or tutors to use with their children at home.

The subject of tutoring is one that will run and run – until a different way of seeing if a child is suitable to enter a grammar school comes into place.

Before we look at the three possible options for tutoring, it is worth mentioning that the tutoring industry has grown at a phenomenal speed over the last ten years. Some experts say that it is now a multi-billion pound industry with tutors being employed to teach children from a very young age right through to eighteen plus. The main thing for parents to note about the tutoring industry at present is that it is completely unregulated. In other words any person can set up as a tutor or start their own tutoring agency, whether they have teaching qualifications or not.

So it is vital that you as a parent find out all you can about your tutor before taking them on. At the very least your tutor should be a qualified teacher and as such should have experience of teaching in a school. Don't be afraid to ask to see their teaching certificate and CV. Also if they are not currently teaching in a school, find out why. Are they retired? Or have they left teaching to do tutoring full time? You could also get in contact with the school where your tutor is/was a teacher to see if they can vouch for their competence.

The other important thing any tutor worth his or her salt will have is either a DBS or a CRB certificate. DBS stands for Disclosure and Barring Service and has recently taken over the older Criminal Records Bureau. This is a government organisation that keeps a check on any person working with or coming into contact with children. If a person has any previous criminal convictions, (including ones against children), this will be shown on the certificate. Usually a school will have these for all their teachers and other staff. Naturally if your potential tutor has one of these certificates, you would expect it to be blank. If the tutor cannot supply one of these when you ask, it might be a good idea to avoid taking him or her on.

So now that has been covered, what are the three ways of tutoring available to a parent?

Private Tuition Centres

The first option is sending your child to an after school establishment where children are tutored in small groups. They are most commonly known as "Education Centres" or "Tuition Centres" and can be found in most towns around the country. The majority of them are not just for 11+ tuition though, but include tuition for SATs and GCSEs as well as basic Maths and English for younger children.

Many of them are in High Streets next to other shops. Some can be found in supermarkets, in rooms attached to the main building. Others might be in church halls or community centres. They are mostly run by ex-teachers or serving teachers, who have either taken out a franchise to operate the centre, or started it from scratch themselves. A lot of the work will be done on a computer and it may be that the ratio of child to teacher could be one to five or even greater.

Things to consider

Cost – How much will they charge for the lesson? Do you have to pay in advance for a block of lessons or can you pay as you go? Can you get a refund if your child misses a lesson? It may well be cheaper than paying for a private tutor, but what is the teacher to pupil ratio? How much 'one to one' attention will your child get?

Curriculum – Do they follow a particular curriculum or lesson plan that all children follow? Or is there scope to cater for your child's particular strengths/weaknesses? For instance, if your child is strong in Maths, but weak in English, will they concentrate on their English needs more? How much work will be done on the computer? Do they use photocopied 11+ practice papers or do they make up their own papers? Do they set homework?

Staffing – What can you find out about the tutors working at your local centre? Are they fully qualified teachers? Can you find out which schools they have taught at, or are still teaching at? Have they been police checked and can they show you a DBS or CRB certificate? Are they insured?

Building – Do they have the relevant insurances in place, particularly public liability insurance? What about fire escapes? Is the furniture up to scratch?

Other things to consider - Are you confident that your child will be safe working there? What are the other children like in your child's group? Are any of them likely to be disruptive? Are any of the staff trained in first aid? How easy is it to park at the centre? Is there a separate waiting area for you to stay whilst the lesson is taking place? Are they flexible waiting for you if you get delayed? What hours are they open? Some open only after school during the week, whilst some open at weekends as well.

Of course with some of the points raised above, you won't really know what it's going to be like until your child actually has a lesson there. Any tuition centre worth using should be able to let your child have a trial lesson to see if he/she likes it and is comfortable with the place. Some centres might let you do this for free, but most will charge for this.
Maybe you already know of another parent who is already using the tuition centre. If you could ask them about what it's like, this may put your mind at ease.

Private Tutors

The second option for you is employing a private tutor. Nowadays it seems almost a given that the majority of children taking the 11+ exam will have tutoring by a private tutor. There are positives and negatives with having a tutor which we will now look at in more detail.

On the plus side, the majority of parents find that having a tutor boosts their child's confidence going into the 11+. Having to face such a difficult exam at a young age is quite daunting for the average ten year old and having a tutor makes the test seem less daunting. A tutor should be knowledgeable about both the subjects taken and the types of questions set. They should be to help your child understand what is expected of them in the 11+ and so help them to sit the tests without any anxiety or nerves. They should also be able to help your child overcome any particular weaknesses with the different types of questions set.

Looking at the negatives, having a tutor doesn't come cheap. Most tutors can charge anything between £20 and £40 per hour for a lesson. (In London this can be as much as £50 per hour). Over several months or even years, this can turn out to be quite a large financial commitment. Are you prepared to pay out such large sums of money, especially when you know your child isn't guaranteed a pass in the 11+ exam?
Then there is the commitment of your time and your child's time. Having a tutor involves a weekly (or twice weekly) lesson which needs a commitment from both parties. Is your child prepared for this commitment? Will they be happy to sit down for an hour each week after a long day at school, or at the weekends when they could be doing something else? It might mean foregoing an after school activity such as a sport's club or a music lesson to fit the 11+ lesson in. Also both you and your child need to be happy with the tutor, otherwise you could be wasting your money. Plus, as mentioned above, having a tutor doesn't mean your child will automatically pass the 11+.

How to find a tutor

Presuming you decide to go ahead with private tuition for your child, how do you go about it? Where can you find a decent, well respected and experienced tutor?

The first and possibly safest way is through word of mouth. Is there anyone you know who has used a tutor in the past? Perhaps ask a parent in the year above your child at school? Can they vouch for his or her competence? Usually a good tutor will be in demand, so it might be worth approaching the tutor a few months in advance of when you will need him/her. Many good tutors do have waiting lists, so the sooner you get in contact, the sooner you can book his/her services.

Secondly, you could ask your child's head teacher if they can nominate anyone they know. It might not necessarily be a teacher at your child's school, but perhaps someone who has worked there in the past, or someone who the head teacher knows personally.

Finally, there are plenty of tuition agencies on line, who can provide the names and contact details of tutors in your area, often with testimonials from previous pupils/parents. Any good tutoring agency will have vetted their tutors, both for competence and for their backgrounds/experience. See the links section at the end of this book for a list of tutoring agencies.

You could also find tutors advertising their services in adverts in newsagent's windows or in local newspapers. Please note that with these there is no way of knowing whether a tutor will be suitable, unless you try them out. Again it would be advisable to check their background and experience before employing them.

Meet with the tutor first

Before you employ any tutor, it is always worth meeting with them first, or at least speaking to them on the telephone. You might like to ask them what teaching experience they have, how long they have been tutoring, whether they have a CRB/DBS certificate they can show you, how much they charge and what days and times they are available. It might be tempting to ask them what their success rate is, but this is a difficult question to answer as some tutors will only take on children they know will pass the 11+, whilst others may take on children regardless of their ability.

When will the lessons take place? Most tutors tend to work straight after school, between the hours of 4.00 to 5.00 pm, or 5.00 to 6.00 pm. Some work later, though many parents feel that their children might be too tired to work that late in the evening. Some do work at weekends which might suit some parents better. So this is something that you need to work out between you and the tutor, especially if you have other children that might be involved in other after school activities.

Other things you should discuss are whether the tutor is prepared to take lessons in the school holidays, if you wish. If your child is ill, or going to a party, or going on a school trip, will you still have to pay the tutor? Some local authorities suggest drawing up a written contract between you and the tutor covering all these eventualities. Most parents prefer the "contract" between themselves and the tutor to be more informal, such as a verbal contract, but it is still important for both parties to be clear on all these issues.

If you are not happy with your tutor for whatever reason, you can choose to stop the lessons.

Where do the lessons take place?

A few tutors have the lessons in their own homes, though most will come to your house to have the lesson. If you have a tutor who works in his/her own home, it would be worth considering whether you would be happy to leave your child there for an hour each week? Perhaps they have another room there where you can wait? Also, can you visit his/her house before you decide to go ahead?

If you have the tutor coming to your house, it is important that you have a suitable room available where the lesson can take place. This might be in your kitchen or dining room, where there is a table available. Or it could be in a lounge, though having lessons sitting on a settee is not an ideal situation. It should not be in a bedroom for obvious reasons.

It is also important that there should be no noise or distractions from things like the TV, the radio, the washing machine, dogs, cats, younger brothers or sisters, people talking in the next room, or people talking on the telephone.

As it is your house, it is up to you whether to leave the door to the room shut or open. Though again, if there is outside noise coming into the room this can be distracting for both your child and the tutor.

The tutor usually should provide all the teaching materials needed, including work sheets, as well as set homework each week. Some tutors however do ask parents to buy a particular workbook or set of papers, which they may use in the lesson.

It goes without saying that the tutor should be teaching for most of the lesson and not just marking previous homework whilst your child twiddles their thumbs. At the end of each lesson he/she should go through with you what your child has covered/learnt that week. Check that they have given you a full hour's worth of their time. If they are late arriving, do they add that missing time on at the end?

One more thing. On no account should you leave your child alone with the tutor whilst you go off to pick up another sibling. The tutor is not a baby sitter and if you ever got delayed or were in an accident, what would happen then?

Stick with one tutor!

I have also come across parents, who in their desperation for their child to pass the 11+ actually employ two different tutors! Not only is this a silly idea, but quite likely your child could end up doing the same pieces of work with both tutors, or even get confused with the different teaching approaches that two tutors may have. This is not a good idea and sounds like desperation on the part of the parent. No, stick to one tutor. You could always increase the amount of lessons the nearer you get to the 11+ if you and the tutor both agree that this is worth doing. Plus your child can still do work with you as well as the tutor, as long as the tutor is aware of this and can advise you on which areas/topics to cover.

On line tutoring

If you find the cost of paying for a private tutor is just too much for you, you could consider trying the services of an on-line tutor. This is a fairly new phenomenon which started with on-line tutoring for Secondary age children and has moved down to the 11+ age group. It is particularly helpful if you live out in the countryside and find it hard to get to a tutor's house or vice-versa. How much interaction there is between your child and the tutor depends on the tutor themselves, but with the advent of web cameras, Skype and FaceTime, this has become much easier to do. Again you might need to keep a tight watch on what is going on to check everything is as you would expect.

Be aware though that some so called on-line tuition websites are more of a course based website, where every child follows a set curriculum and everything is programmed in. The one-to-one tuition for your child that you were expecting, may well just be a computer programme, as opposed to a real person.

Tip: Try searching for "on-line 11+ tutors" on the internet and see what comes up. Or ask in one of the various 11+ forums to see if anyone can recommend a suitable website. The links to the various forums can be found at the end on the book in the chapter called "11+ Links".

Do it yourself tuition at home

The third option is that of teaching your child yourself at home. If you take the route of teaching your child at home your self, you will need to be quite strict about how often you approach the whole learning process. If you just give your child a practice paper to attempt and then leave him/her to get on with it, whilst you carry out another task in the house, you will be defeating the object of the exercise.

It is also important that you are capable of understanding the various concepts, methods and types of questions that you get in the 11+ exam. If this is beyond you, then it is obviously not for you. Also it is only going to work if your child is prepared to sit down for an hour a week with you and actually work. If they won't "buckle down" for you, then it is not going to work. One compromise to this situation might be to get a grandparent, or aunt or uncle to take over this role. They will know your child, but not be as close to them as you would be.

Tip: There are plenty of on-line lessons about the various types of questions types that come up in the 11+ to be found on internet sites such as "You Tube". These have an 11+ expert showing you the parent, "how to do" the different types of questions, often with diagrams to make it easier to understand. These can be quite useful in preparing for the 11+.

Finally, there is another form of "tuition" (if you can call it that), which has started in the past few years. That is when the grammar schools themselves have "taster days" for year 5 children (usually in their feeder school area), where they spend a morning or even a whole day at the grammar school doing some practice for the 11+. This has consisted of going through and then attempting a mock 11+ paper in some or all of the subjects which they test, so that the children can get a feel for the school and the test itself. From what I have heard, the children find it quite a relaxing time and it helps them to see what the 11+ is all about.

Not all grammar schools do this though and it usually organised via your child's primary school. So if you are not sure if this happens with the grammar schools in your area, maybe you could ring the grammar school direct to see if they do have one these taster days.

Keep in touch with the tutor

Once the tuition has finished and your child has taken the 11+, don't forget about the tutor! It is common courtesy to let the tutor know how your son or daughter got on in the 11+, whether they made the grade or not. They too will be just as keen as you are to find out your child's result. They might also be useful in helping you to decide what to do next should your child fail to reach the entry score for a particular school. Also, you might want the same tutor to tutor a younger brother or sister a few years down the line. It never ceases to amaze me that the occasional parent doesn't bother to let their tutor know how their child got on the 11+!

In the next chapter I will go into more detail about what you as a parent should be doing in the time leading up to the 11+, including what to do on the day itself.

CHAPTER 7 – THE PERIOD LEADING UP TO THE 11+

In this chapter I will go over what you as a parent should be doing at what stage of the school year, as well giving you some advice on how to get the most out of the 11+ for your child. Some of this has been touched on earlier, but it is important that you as a parent are sure of what you should be doing and when.

The year leading up to the 11+ test

At least a year before the 11+ exams take place, you should be starting to think seriously about the 11+ and your choice of secondary school for your child. The first thing to decide is whether you would like your child to attend a grammar school or not. You also need to be sure that s/he is academically capable of coping with the exam and a grammar school education afterwards. If so, you need to look at the different grammar schools that are in your area and within a reasonable travelling distance as well. Some children have journeys of an hour each way to and from their grammar school. Seriously consider if this is an option you would like for your child. Also consider which secondary school your child would go to if they were unsuccessful in the 11+ exam.

Make sure that you are clear when the closing dates for forms to be returned to the various grammar schools are, as well as the open days/evenings where you and your child go to see inside the grammar school. What work are you going to do with them at home in the months leading up to the 11+ exam? Are you going to send them to a tuition centre for extra lessons? Or are you going to employ a tutor to help your child prepare for the 11+ exam? Or perhaps you will be doing all the preparation work yourself? Also worth thinking about is whether you would like your child to attend a "mock 11+ test" day? Some grammar schools now have these, as well as private tuition companies, so it pays to check with the grammar school if they provided this option. See below for more information.

Above all, it is important that you formulate a plan of the way forward for your child, which includes the work s/he will be doing in the months leading up to the 11+, as well as which schools you will be applying for.

The final few months before the 11+

This time is probably the most important part of preparing your child for the 11+. By now your child should be in a routine with the work they do at home, whether it is set by their tutor (if they have one), or you. This is when all the "meaty" stuff should be done, such as making sure they are competent in all the various mathematical concepts that they need to know, or the different types of Verbal Reasoning questions. Help them to see where they are weak in certain areas and with encouragement from you (and their tutor), they should be able to overcome these weaknesses.

As I mentioned before, don't overdo it. Keep a balance between work and leisure, so that their brain gets a break from time to time. A day off each week from 11+ preparation is worth considering. Sometimes schoolwork can get in the way of their 11+ preparation and may seem completely irrelevant to the looming exam. Try not to get too uptight about this, but see it as a type of preparation in that they are still learning something and exercising their brains.

It is also important at this stage that they learn about the possible mistakes and pitfalls that most children make when they sit the 11+ exam. I have made a list below of what I consider the most common mistakes children make during the exam. If your child can learn and understand these at this stage, they will not be so stressed on the day and will get higher marks than those who are not prepared.

Top 10 errors made by children during the 11+ exam

1) Not reading the question properly.
2) Spending too much time trying to answer a question.
3) Not showing your working out in Maths.
4) Copying down the answer incorrectly from a working out.
5) Writing down incorrect spellings in the English exam.
6) Missing out a question or even a whole section.
7) Not drawing a true horizontal line across the box in a multiple choice based exam.
8) Not reading the mathematical sign properly. E.g. thinking it's an addition sum when it's a division sum.
9) Not interpreting a word sum/problem properly to work out the answer.
10) Putting the answer in the wrong place. E.g. outside the answer box.

In addition, I would add illegible hand writing to the above, as the other thing which loses children marks in the 11+. So try and encourage your child to write their answers neatly and clearly.

I have also added an extra chapter at the end of this book called "11+ Advice and Hints" which goes into more detail about all these possible pitfalls in the 11+ exam.

11+ Stress

I have known some children at this stage, who suddenly find that it's all too much and they mentally start going to pieces. Some just need a break from all their work, whilst others decide that the 11+ and all the stress involved is not for them. If this does happen to your child, you will need to seriously think whether to continue or not. Speak to your child's class teacher and head teacher to see what they think and do talk things through with your child in case it is some other factor that is affecting them. Sometimes it is the parents who feel it is all too much stress and bother and make this decision not to continue. Again it is imperative that you speak with someone who can advise you in making this decision. If you do decide to not continue, you will need to let the grammar school(s) that you have applied to, know about your decision.

Whilst all children can get stressed with the 11+ plus, most accept it as part and parcel of life. It's a hurdle that they have to get over. The rise of social media in the past few years can also add to a child's 11+ stress. The increase of the use of mobile phones by children, as well as the internet can also cause stress, as one child's ideas about the 11+ can be passed round the whole class. So keep on eye on this. Has something someone has said about the 11+ upset your child? Nerves leading up to the exam are quite natural. So it is important that you as a parent are sensitive to your child's feelings and emotions at this time. Be prepared to listen to their fears about the 11+. Are they justified? Or are they the result of someone spreading false rumours?

Some parents go down the alternative health route and try things such as homeopathic medicines, NLP (Neuro-linguistic Programming) or other alternative therapies as ways to reduce their child's nerves. Others try bribery in the form of promising a big reward if they pass the 11+. Personally I am against this, as it can easily backfire if the child isn't successful in the 11+. Also, what happens at the next set of exams? Many parents doing this can make a rod for their own backs. How do you motivate your child then? If a child is taking the 11+, it should be because a) they want to and b) they are academically up to it. By all means give them a reward after the exam has been taken, or after the results come out, but not as a carrot to get them to work harder.

11+ Mock days

Over the past few years "11+ Mock days" have sprung up in most areas where the 11+ exam takes place. They are designed to give the child a taste of what a real 11+ exam is like, complete with various exam papers to do under timed conditions in an unfamiliar setting. Many parents book a place hoping that the experience will boost their child's confidence and give them an advantage when it comes to the real 11+ test.

However, I would urge caution when considering whether to put your child down for one of these Mock 11+ test days. Before you go ahead, you need to be happy with the people who are organising the event. Do you know anything about them? Have they been CRB/DBS checked and is there proper insurance in place for the building and in case of accidents? After all, you are handing your child over to some strangers for a few hours, without you being there. As with lots of things to do with the 11+, there are positives and negatives with 11+ Mock Days.

On the plus side, your child will have the pressure of completing one or more 11+ tests under timed conditions. They will probably be in a strange building and will be mixing with other children that they don't know. So the idea is that they won't be so stressed or nervous when they sit the actual 11+ exam, as they will have done it all before.

On the negative side, you might find that just a handful of children turn up to take the mock test, when you were expecting a large room full of children. So the experience for your child might not be as big a test as you hoped for. You could enquire before you commit, as to how many children are signed up if you are concerned about this. Also, you might find that the tests they use are just photocopied from practice papers that your child may have already attempted at home or at school. So your child might not be being tested with new unseen questions and you will be wasting your money. Again it might be worth checking with the organisers whether they make up new questions for the tests or not.

Finally, by far the biggest negative is the results. If your child doesn't do that well in the tests, it can be very demoralising for your child and can upset their momentum going into the 11+. I have known several children who have taken a mock 11+ test in the past, who have achieved low scores, who then feel that they will not pass the 11+, so it is both a battle for their parents and tutors to convince them otherwise.

Tip: Whether you send your child to a mock 11+ exam or not, you can still get your son/daughter to do a mock 11+ exam at home if you wish. This is a good way of showing to your child just how quickly the time goes in exam conditions, as well as what it is like to complete two/three exams all in quick succession. I would suggest doing this at home one Saturday morning about two or three weeks to the day (if possible) before the actual 11+ exam. Make sure that you are able to commit to the two or three hours needed to complete the tests. If possible, set the subjects in the same order as the real 11+ exam, with suitable breaks in between.

You should also make sure your child is not disturbed by things such as telephones, pets and other siblings. You could use previous practice papers that have been attempted before if you don't want to stress him/her out too much. Remember the aim is to get your child used to the time constraints and the need to work quickly and accurately.

Summer Holidays

Almost every child taking the 11+ exam in England has to take the exam just a few weeks after the end of the summer holidays. I am often asked by parents whether I think it is OK for the family to take a holiday during this time or should they stay at home to concentrate on 11+ revision? I always advise parents that a holiday is a good thing for both you and your children. After all, a break from work can help recharge the batteries. I would advise you to go on holiday earlier than later in the summer holiday period if possible, though of course it is up to the parents when you choose to go.

If you do go on holiday, do you have a complete break from revision or do you take work with you for your child to do? From my experience, it is very hard to get a child to sit down and get on with school work/revision when they are in holiday mode. So if you do decide to take revision work away with you, try and keep it low key and don't make too much of an issue if your child refuses to complete it. The important time is when you are home after the holiday, getting back into the swing of things with 11+ revision. The date of the 11+ will soon creep up on you, so make sure you are using all that holiday time for the final weeks of revision to your child's advantage.

The week leading up to the 11+ test

Once the new term starts, the remaining weeks before the 11+ will fly past, and before you know it 11+ Day will have arrived. In the week leading up to the 11+, I would avoid letting your child go to a sleepover or going away for the weekend. Anything out of the ordinary just before the 11+ test, can affect your child's sleep pattern and it is important that they stay in a normal school routine in the final days leading up to the 11+ test day. If the test is on a Saturday, children will find it harder than those who take it during the week, mainly because they will have had five full schooldays beforehand. Therefore, you as parents need to make sure that they are in their best physical shape possible. This includes keeping to a regular sleep pattern, as well as eating the best energy giving foods available.

Work wise, I would say concentrate on any areas of the 11+ curriculum that your child is still unsure of, rather than doing any practice papers. Keep the work you do at home light at this late stage, so that they have plenty of mental energy ready to be used in the exam itself. Things like parts of speech or Maths equivalents are the sort of things that might need reinforcing at this stage. The main focus of your child's 11+ preparation should be over by now.

Tip: As it is always busy traffic wise on the morning of the 11+ exam outside the grammar school, it might be worthwhile you making a reconnaissance trip sometime in the week before the exam. That way you will be sure of the route you have to take, how long the journey takes and you can see where the best parking places are. If you are lucky, the grammar school might have a car park for parents within its grounds. If not, it might be easier to park a little way from the school, rather than on top of it and walk some of the way. A little fresh air before the exam can do your child the world of good.

The night before

Try and be as low key as possible. It is not a good idea to get your child to do a practice paper so late in the day. If they don't know what to do by now, why are they sitting the 11+? The important thing is to keep them relaxed and calm. So let them watch their normal TV programmes or play on their computer. If they have a club like cubs or guides I would err on the side of caution as to whether they should go or not. If they are likely to go to bed later than on a normal school day, it might be best to miss that one.

Try not to talk about the exam unless your child brings the subject up. Make sure you reassure them that it will be fine and that you will be proud of them whatever the result. If you do start talking about the exam, this can only add to their nerves and concerns about the exam and stop them from having a good night's sleep.

Tip: On the night before the 11+, you could also make sure that you have any pens/pencils/rubbers/pencil sharpeners ready and handy for in the morning, as well as your paperwork that you need for entry to the school. Other things might be glasses or an inhaler, or a mascot. Some schools allow children to take in mascots, some don't. Your child might find having a mascot comforting, but it is best to make sure if they allowed, from the school beforehand. Also find out they are allowed to take snacks and drinks in with them. If so, have these ready as well.

The day of the 11+

Make sure you all get up in plenty of time, so that you are not rushing. For breakfast, give your child something that is going to sustain them through the morning, such as porridge or fruit, such as a banana or an apple, rather than a biscuit or chocolate. Obviously if your child is a fussy eater and will not eat healthy food, I suppose some food is better than no food at all. Some children will say they are not hungry and it will be tempting to let them get away without eating anything. This can only lead to fainting and hunger pangs in the exam, so try and get them to eat something.

If you are driving to the school, make sure you leave in plenty of time to find a parking space. It is better to be there in good time and arrive relaxed at the school gates, rather than rushing at the last minute and getting stressed trying to find somewhere to park. I have known the police to be called out at some schools to control the traffic – not the parents! – as it can get very busy, especially if two or three schools are near each other. If you do have time to kill, go over some times tables, spellings or word games which will help "warm up" your child's brain, so to speak. Don't go on about what to do or not to do in the test; it will only add to their stress. Make sure you have the various pieces of paperwork needed as well as your child's pens, pencils, rubber and ruler ready.

When you get to the school it can seem like chaos has erupted with parents and their children coming from all directions. You might see children crying, or even being sick, which is how some children react to the pressure of the 11+ test in extreme cases. Whether you decide to warn your child about this beforehand is up to you, as you know your child best and how they might react to a situation like this. Above all try and keep them calm and focussed on their task. Some parents "gee up" their children by likening the 11+ to a race that they are about to run in, or a military battle that they are about to fight, or a mountain that they are going to climb. Other parents just see it as part of growing up and let them get on with it.

You have done all you can do. The rest is up to your child now. Go home and try and take your mind off what your child is going through – if you can! Maybe do some shopping, or go for a walk, or read a book. If you are allowed to stay in the school, it can get rather tense and claustrophobic with all those parents talking about the 11+, so I would advise you to go away and come back at the end if you possibly can.

What if my child is ill on the day of the 11+ test?

If your child is genuinely ill, it is important that you make the decision not to let your child take the 11+ test that day, as early as possible. You should ring the school where your child is due to take the exam as soon as possible. All grammar schools will have a reserve date for children in these circumstances. You should also notify your doctor, so you can get a medical certificate/letter proving that your child was genuinely unwell and so not able to take the exam that day. Most grammar schools will ask to see a doctor's certificate to prove that your child was ill.

Very occasionally, a child might injure themselves, perhaps in a game of sport in the days leading up to the 11+. They might need crutches to walk, or even a wheel chair to get about in. The grammar school should be notified immediately if this happens, so arrangements can be made for the school to cater for the child. If a child injures his or her writing hand and finds it difficult to hold a pen or even write, the grammar school may provide an adult who will write down the answers for the child. Not the best way to attempt an 11+ exam I know, but better than nothing. Again, the school should be notified as soon as possible. In a case like this, your child may be allowed to wait until the reserve date to take the test, when their hand might have healed up more.

Another thing which may affect a child in the 11+ is that of bereavement, whether it be their favourite pet, or a relative such as a grandparent. In the latter case your child might be able to take the test on the reserve day, but again I would speak to someone at the grammar school if you think it might affect their performance.

You can of course write to the grammar school after the exam to say that this event may have affected their score, but whether they would take this into consideration or not is up to the grammar school. It is also something that you could mention if you had to appeal at a later date.

Once the 11+ exam has finished

When the children come out of the 11+ exam it will be very tempting for you to want to know how they got on. Try and hold back if possible and let your child "open up" to you about what it was like, rather than you or your partner interrogating them about every aspect of the exam. You may have to wait an hour or so after the exam, once your child has settled down after such a stressful few hours. It is very easy to draw conclusions about how they have done from what they say and many parents often jump to the unnecessary conclusion that they have "failed". This is something you will have to try and put to the back of your mind for the next few weeks, as you really won't know until the grammar school gives out its results.

On the day of the exam, once it is all over, some parents like to take their son/daughter out to lunch as a treat, or even to the cinema, or to a sporting event. This will only suit some children, as other children will be so shattered by the 11+ experience that they would rather just chill out at home watching the TV or playing games on their computer. Once again this is something that you will need to decide for yourselves, or even play it according to how your child feels on the day.

You yourself will no doubt feel a great sense of relief now that it is all over - or the first part at least! At the same time, you may feel anxious as the day for the 11+ results draws nearer. At least nowadays it is only a few weeks to wait, rather than a few months. Now is the time for getting on with your life after all the stress of the last year. You should have some more "me" time for yourself, whilst your child may be ready to take up the sport or hobby that fell by the wayside with all that 11+ preparation going on.

Tip: It might be a good idea to start putting some money away in a savings account ready for all the costs associated with your child starting his/her new secondary school. This will soon creep up on you, so if you have some money put aside for this, the shock of the costs involved won't be as great. There is more information on this in the next chapter.

In the next chapter I will discuss what happens in the period after the 11+ and your child going to secondary school.

CHAPTER 8 – THE PERIOD AFTER THE 11+

In this final chapter I will explain what happens once the 11+ is over and how to go about making the best decisions regarding you child's transition from primary to secondary school and after.

11+ Results Day

As discussed earlier, you will be informed sometime in October (in most cases) by the grammar school(s) as to what score your child will have achieved in the 11+, rather than whether s/he has passed or not. You will have a choice of finding out by letter or by e-mail. Most parents nowadays choose the e-mail option as that seems quicker in most cases. I think it is a good idea to open the letter or e-mail together as parent and child, rather than keeping the result from your child. Once you have taken in the contents of the e-mail/letter, it will be a time for celebration or for consoling your child.

If it is the latter result, it can be a harrowing experience for both you and your child. Your son/daughter might be quite upset at first, but children do bounce back. So try and encourage them to think towards their new school in a positive way, rather than look back to what might have been. Whatever school they are going to, that is the best one for them.

Tip: It might be very tempting if your child was successful in the 11+, to ring round to tell his/her friends about their result. But what if their friend's result was different than your child's? It could cause more upset. Also, what if your child wasn't successful in gaining a high enough mark? Would you want other children ringing your child up, who were successful? Perhaps, arrange beforehand with the parents of your child's friends, what you will do on result's day, so that you don't inadvertently cause more distress.

You now have to start thinking about your child's options ready for filling out the Common Application Form based upon your child's results If your child reached the required score, you can go ahead and put that school as your number one choice. If your child reached a "borderline" score, either just above or just below the minimum score, you can still put that grammar school as your number one choice, but be prepared that s/he isn't guaranteed a place. So have your alternative school down for your second choice. Finally, if your child's score was below the minimum score by some points, you must accept that s/he will not be going to grammar school in September and so your number one choice may well be your first choice comprehensive school.

Make sure you get the form in to your local education authority by 31st October. Then you have another four months of waiting until you hear exactly what school your child has been allocated a place at for the following September.

National Results Day

As mentioned earlier, the day that the allocations of Secondary schools come out is called National Results Day (or National Secondary Schools Allocation Day) and is normally on 1st March. You will then find out which secondary school your child has been offered a place at. If it is your first choice, you will no doubt be very happy and can finally get on with your life.

If it is not your first choice, you will have to decide whether to accept this offer or go into appeal mode. Usually you will have around three weeks whether to accept or reject the offer.

Appeals

There are two reasons why parents appeal against the decision not to award their child a place at a grammar school. The first reason is when the grammar school is oversubscribed and so the child may have reached the required score, but has been refused a place due to other criteria, such as distance from the school or precedence being given to children with other siblings at the school.

The second and more common reason is when the child did not reach the required score, due to being unable to do their best in the tests, such as being affected by bereavement in the family, or being distracted by another child in the exam room, for example.

If you feel strongly that your child should have been offered a place at your first choice grammar school and is academically capable, then you have the right to appeal. You could also at this stage ask to be put on the school's waiting list, if the school doesn't automatically do this.

It is important that you look at all the pros and cons of this process and only if you think that you have a realistic chance, should you proceed with your appeal. Just to show you how difficult it is to succeed at the appeal stage, here are some figures of appeals for the Southend grammar schools from 2013. For the four selective grammar schools there were initially sixty appeals. Straight away, ten of these were rejected as being unsuitable before going to appeal. Of the fifty cases that did go to appeal, just two were accepted. So the chances of being successful at an appeal are very slim in most areas.

If you are determined to appeal, the first person you should consult is your child's head teacher, who will either encourage you to go ahead if they think it is worth appealing, or tell you not to proceed if they think you don't have a realistic chance. Their support is crucial in your appeal. From then on, you can choose to go it alone or you can get professional help from an educational consultant or a specialist solicitor.

Tip: If you type in the phrase "11+ appeals" in your search engine, you will be sure to find a whole host of people advertising their services of helping parents through the appeals process. Before employing their services, it would be advisable to see what testimonials (if any) they have and find out how much they charge and just what advice they can offer you.

What an appeal entails

Usually, when you appeal against a grammar school's decision not to award a place to your child, there are certain things that you have to do when making an appeal. You might like to find out about the School Admissions Appeals Code which came into force in 2012. This has led to a more robust appeals process which is legally binding and sets out all the various rules, regulations and obligations of the schools and appeals panels. The link to this document is as follows:-

https://www.gov.uk/government/uploads/system/uploads/attachment_data/file/389388/School_Admissions_Code_2014_-_19_Dec.pdf

You should let your local education authority know that you will be appealing against the decision. Make sure you do this before the closing date. You don't have to include your reasons yet. This can be done at a later date. When you do write a letter supporting your appeal, there are various pieces of evidence you can present. This might be your child's school results like SATs tests, school reports and comments. If possible get a supporting letter or comments from your child's head teacher and class teacher backing up your case. It is not a good idea to mention a private tutor's opinion as this might go against you. There are other things that you can include, such as your child's extra curricular activities, their hobbies and the clubs they attend.

Tip: There are plenty of articles on the internet in which parents write about their experiences of going through an appeal. They often suggest other reasons used in appeals which you might not have thought of, so do an internet search to see what other arguments you could put forward.

Once the school has received the appeal letter and documentation from you, there will be a gap before you hear if your application for an appeal has been accepted or rejected. If it has been accepted you will be given a date for the appeal.

At the appeal you will have to face a panel of around three to five appeals' panellists. These should be independent of the grammar school but at least one should be familiar with the processes involved. You (or your nominated spokesperson) will be required to state your case. It might be quite daunting to do this, so having spent some time practising what you have to say beforehand will help ease your nerves. Don't just read out what you have written in your letter, but have a more concise version ready, which will be more acceptable to the panel, who may have heard dozens of appeals before yours. You should be prepared to argue your case, so have back up answers ready and try not to get too emotional as you speak. You will then have to wait several days or weeks before you find out what the panel's decision is.

In some areas, whole groups of parents who are appealing are called in before a panel as a "group appeal" and are then told why there are no places for their children. Parents can ask questions and argue their case to the local authority representatives, but it is up to the appeals panel to decide how many children will be admitted or not admitted.

Eventually, you will hear whether your appeal has been successful or not. If it has, you can be grateful and pleased with yourself that it has all been worth it. If it hasn't, you may well feel quite down, with a strong feeling of rejection for the second time in a few months. You must now decide whether you will accept the school that the local authority offered you, or start looking at other options, which I discussed in Chapter 3.

Getting ready for Secondary school

Once things have settled down after National Results Day and you know which secondary school your child will be going to, it is a good idea to start thinking ahead about getting your child ready for the start of their secondary school days.

Most secondary schools, be they grammar or comprehensive, nowadays have an induction day where the new Year 7 intake spend a morning or even a whole day at their new school. This gives the child a chance to learn about the school, such as where the classrooms and subject rooms are situated and what the timetable will be like.

Even if they don't do this, the grammar school still might send a year 7 teacher over to the child's primary school to meet the new intake there. The year 7 teacher will liaise with the year 6 teacher(s) about the new pupils and which children might be better kept apart or put in the same class as is the case.

Tip: If you are concerned about your son/daughter settling down in their new school, you could always write to, or ring the head of Year 7 with your concerns. I know of some parents who ask that their child be put in the same class as one of their friends from primary school, so that they have someone they were familiar with to help them settle in quicker. If you choose to do this, do it sooner than later, as class allocations can take place fairly soon after the places have been allocated. Please be aware that this is not guaranteed, as it really is up to the grammar school to decide who goes where.

The cost of Secondary school education

One of the most important ways in which you as a parent can be prepared for Secondary School is to have enough money put by to pay for the new school uniform and all the paraphernalia that goes with it. If you have been sensible, you will have put aside a certain amount of money each week/month to pay for all of these.

Here is an example of what a parent might have to spend on school uniform for a Year 7 child when s/he first enters Secondary school. Please note that these are approximate prices and may well vary from school to school.

Blazer - £60.00
Trousers/Skirts - £20.00
Shirts - £15.00
Jumpers - £18.00
Socks - £2.50
Shoes - £40.00
Tie(s) - £5.00
Lab. Coat - £17.00

PE Top - £9.00
PE Shorts - £5.00
Tracksuit - £44.00
Sports Socks - £2.00

TOTAL: £237.50

This does not include extra pairs of trousers/skirts/shirts/socks, etc which could bring the total to over £300!

Apart from the school uniform above, parents will also be expected to buy at least some of the following school items:-

Maths calculator - £14.50
Safety glasses for Science - £3.00
Bible - £9.00
English Dictionary - £9.00
French Dictionary - £7.00
Thesaurus - £4.00
Games kit bag - £15.00
Boot bag - £7.50
Shin guards - £5.00
Gum shield - £2.50
Security bag - £2.50

TOTAL: £79.00

The total of all the above is now over £300, so if you have a child in year 6 it might be worth saving up now!

It doesn't end there though! Other costs to take into consideration could include:

School meals for each school day
A contribution to the school fund
Name tapes to label all your child's clothes and property
Bus/train fares if your child lives some way from the school
Bicycle and helmet if s/he decides to cycle to school

Sport's equipment such as a hockey stick, or a tennis racket

Plus: costs of school trips throughout the year

You might be able to save on the costs of some items by buying at a high street department store or off the internet, rather than at a dedicated school uniform shop. It is worth remembering though that most grammar schools have their own uniform shop, where you have to buy certain items which cannot be bought elsewhere, such as the school blazer and tie. It is also worth buying the uniform sooner than later, as stock can be used up in the rush by the new intake.

Tip: If money is tight and your child doesn't mind, you can consider buying things like the blazer, the tie and PE kit second hand. Most schools have second hand uniform sales throughout the year, so this might be a way for you to save money. Check with the school website to see when these are.

The end of an era and the start of a new one

So after all the stress and worry of the past year or so, your son or daughter is finally leaving primary school and moving up to secondary school. Whether it is a grammar, comprehensive or private school, the challenges for each child can be the same. You will find that they soon grow up and start to mature as they begin life in senior school. No doubt at first you will be taking a keen interest in all they do, such at what new friends have they made? What homework have they got? What after school clubs are they involved in?

It might be easy to let them get on with it, especially if you yourself are busy with work or other commitments, but I would say it is important that you keep an eye on things, not just at the beginning of their secondary school time, but all the way through it. It is a good idea to know who your point of contacts are at your child's new school, be it their class teacher, head of year, deputy head, head teacher or head of governors.

Most children will not want you interfering in their school lives, but on occasions there might be something that happens to your child at school that causes you concern. It might be bullying, an injury, a detention or something else. Always speak to someone at the school if you have any qualms, rather than letting it build up into something larger. Nip it in the bud while you can. There can be nothing more embarrassing than going along to a parent's evening and being told something about your child's behaviour or work rate that you knew nothing about.

Hopefully your child's time at secondary school will be a happy and fruitful one, with them achieving good grades at both GCSE and A-level. If your child does go to a grammar school, the school would no doubt expect your child to move onto further education, be it University or

Specialist College. So there will be several more years of hard work ahead for your son or daughter. Try and encourage them through the highs and lows of their school lives whatever they may choose to do in life.

So we come to the end of the book. Hopefully what you have read will be helpful in guiding you and your child through the ups and downs of transferring to Secondary education and in particular the 11+. There are two further chapters which give you some other tips and advice when sitting the 11+ exam, as well as many useful links which go into more detail on some of the points raised in this book. Good Luck!

APPENDIX 1 – 11+ EXAM ADVICE AND HINTS

Over the years, I have seen children making the same mistakes, both in their 11+ practise and in the actual exam itself. I have put together a list of hints and advice for children to be aware of when they take the 11+ test. Some are general things applicable to all subjects. Others are applicable to a particular subject. Please note that not every point will be relevant to every area where the 11+ exam takes place.

GENERAL ADVICE:
1) Go to the toilet first before the test starts if at all possible.
2) Don't concern yourself with what other people are doing in the exam. Just concentrate on answering your paper within the allotted time.
3) Make sure you read the question. Don't just look at the example and assume you know what you have to do. Be clear on what you have to do from the instructions.
4) Don't spend too long on a question that you are finding difficult to answer. If you have spent over a minute trying to work out the answer, it is time to move on to the next question. Leave that question out and come back to it later. Put a mark at the side so you can spot it quicker when you come back to it. Sometimes, leaving a hard question and then coming back to it later, makes it easier to do.
5) Write clearly. Make sure that what you write can be read easily by the examiner. This is especially important in English where a badly written answer can lose you marks. Also in Maths, make sure you write your numbers clearly. For both subjects take care with these letters/numbers so that the examiner can see what you have written. The most common errors are usually between these letters and numbers:-
5 and S, 1 and L, D and P, 5 and 8, T and l, 6 and b.
6) If you do make a mistake and want to write in a fresh answer, rub out your mistake (if it is in pencil) and write down the new answer clearly. If you have written in pen, put a line through it and write the answer clearly next to it. Never write a correction over a letter or word where you have made a mistake.
7) If you do finish before the end, go over your answers again. Have you missed any out? Have you miss-spelt any words?
8) Take care not to turn over two pages instead of one and so miss a whole section out.
9) In most areas where the 11+ is taken you are allowed to write your working out and possible answers on the question paper. But make sure you leave a space round the answer box so your answer can be seen clearly.

10) Have your watch nearby, as you will need to keep a close eye on the time, so that you are working to your time schedule. You may well be told by the invigilator when you are half way through and when you have five minutes left. Use this to check if you are on schedule or not.

11) If you are told there are five minutes left, this is the time to fill in any gaps in the answer boxes in the multiple choice type answer papers, and to answer any remaining questions in the standard type papers.

12) If you do finish before the end, check to see you haven't missed any questions out and check that what you have written for each answer is correct.

13) If it is a multiple choice 11+ exam, make sure that you have put a line in every answer box on the answer sheet, as it is very easy to miss putting a line in every box. You might still get a mark even if you are not sure of the answer.

14) Always have a ruler with you, as they are useful for not only drawing straight lines, but also for several other things. In Maths they can help you read the totals of items on block graphs or help you work out lines of symmetry. In English using a ruler to help you read a long passage can help you read every line, rather than miss out a line.

15) Make sure you know whether you are allowed to answer the questions in pen or pencil or either. If it is pencil, always take a spare pencil and a pencil sharpener into the exam room with you – if this is allowed.

ENGLISH ADVICE:

1) If there is a comprehension in your 11+ test, you should read through the passage once at the beginning of the test, so you get an idea of what the passage is about. This should take you between five and ten minutes. If you are still reading through the passage after ten minutes it is time for you to go onto the questions. As you read through the passage, underline any words that you don't understand – with a ruler if possible. This will help you if there is a meaning of words question. Once you have read the passage ask yourself: Who are the main characters? What happens? Where does it take place? This will help you when you answer the questions.

2) Answer the questions that you find easy to answer first of all. Leave any hard questions until after you have answered these.

3) Write all your answers clearly and neatly as an examiner may take off marks for something that can't be read easily.

4) Make sure you know your parts of speech – nouns, verbs, adjectives, adverbs, etc - and the job they do. This will help you if there is a meaning of words question. If the word is a verb, you need to find a word in the

passage that is a verb. If it is an adjective, you will need to find an adjective, etc. Quite often words that end in 'ly' 'ing' or 'ed' will also have their meaning words ending in 'ly' 'ing' or 'ed'

5) Make sure you know the different punctuation marks and what they do. This will help you if there is a punctuation question. Remember to only put speech marks/inverted commas around the words that are spoken, followed by a comma (if it is not the end of a sentence).

6) Do not start an answer with "because". You could lose a mark for this.

7) If there is a meaning of words question, leave this until you have answered all the other questions as this usually takes the most time to answer. Mark on the passage page the section where you are looking for the word. Any words you have underlined, (when you read through the passage at the start), may well be the actual meaning word you are looking for.

8) If you have to create a piece of writing or essay, try and make some notes of what you will include in your writing before you start. This will help you get a clear plan of what you are going to write, as well as help you to remember any important words/actions you want to include in your writing. Always read through what you have written in case of any spelling/grammar errors.

9) If you are answering a comprehension passage, keep the passage in front of you on one side of the desk and the question paper on the other side.

10) If you finish before the end, check to see you haven't missed any questions out and check that what you have written for each answer is correct.

MATHS ADVICE:

1) Go through the test in order, but miss out any hard questions that you are not sure about. Put a dot or cross at the side so you can come back to these at the end.

2) Make sure you read the questions thoroughly and know what you have to do.

3) Take care to do what you are told to do, especially if it is an add, subtract, multiply, divide question. For example, many children do an add sum when it is a subtraction sum, as they haven't looked carefully at the question.

3) Always show your working out for each question if possible. You may still get a mark, even if your answer is wrong.

4) Have a ruler handy so that you can check the levels on bar graphs.

5) Always check your calculations at the end, if you have time. Many marks are lost through making a mistake in these.

6) When writing down a calculation that is in a column, make sure you leave enough space to fit in all the calculation and it doesn't go onto the space for the next question.

7) Don't try and work everything out in your head! Many children do this and get confused, when it is much easier to write down the calculation on the exam paper in front of them. If they get the answer, wrong they may still get a mark for showing the calculation.

NON-VERBAL REASONING ADVICE

1) Make sure you are clear on what the question is asking you to do. If there is an example, look at it, so you can see how the answer works for the question.

2) Always do the easier questions first and leave the harder questions until later. Don't waste time trying to do hard questions. Come back to them later.

3) If you do miss a question out, put a dot or asterisk at the side, so you can easily see where you have a question still to do.

4) When doing an odd one out question, look at the example first to see what you have to do and try and see which boxes have similar or common things in them. You could tick or dot the ones which are in the same group to make it clearer for you.

5) If you are doing a similar pattern question, try and spot what shapes/symbols/line are the same in each box, so you can work out the connection.

6) If you are doing a rotation type question, don't be afraid to rotate your exam paper so you can see which way a shape rotates. Don't hold it up though as other pupils might see it! Keep it flat.

VERBAL REASONING ADVICE:

1) Do the sections you find easier to do first of all. Don't be afraid to leave out whole sections of hard VR questions such as letter sequences or codes, even if they are at the beginning. You will get more marks from answering the questions you can do, rather from attempting the harder questions near the beginning and then running out of time.

2) With FINDING THE MISSING NUMBER FROM THREE NUMBERS always look for a mathematical function. Is it add, minus, multiply or divide? There may be a second function such as times 2 or add 2. You have two examples to work on. If it only works for one of them, you have not found the right formula. So try again.

3) With CODES make sure you understand the different patterns that codes are made up of. The most common are: +1, +1, etc. +2, +2, etc. +1, +2, +3, etc. –1, -1, etc, -2, -2, etc, -1, -2, -3, etc. The harder ones can have both + and – in them. Eg +1, -2, +3, -4. Sometimes the code can be just the word written backwards. Always write the numbers or letters above the code word so you can read it off more easily. Make sure that you know which way you are doing the code. i.e. from word to code, or from code to word.

4) With a 4 LETTER WORD hidden between two words, use two rulers or your fingers as you go along the sentence to see each four-letter word as it appears.

5) With a 3 LETTER WORD hidden in a word, try saying the sentence in your mind to see if you get a better idea of what the word might be. If it is a multiple choice exam, you can look at the answer choices on the answer sheet to see if you get a better idea of the answer.

6) With LOGIC QUESTIONS, such as who came before who, or who wore what, always write down the order of things on the question sheet so you are clear of the order.

7) With COMPOUND WORDS try each different pair of words together until you are sure of the correct answer. Again using the answer box might make this easier for you rather than looking at the question paper.

8) With MISSING LETTERS from the end and start of two words, use the answer sheet to see what five letters are available for the answer. Make sure that the letter you choose fits all four words. If it only fits two or three words, you've got the wrong letter!

9) With NUMBER SEQUENCES make sure you know the number of spaces there are between each letter or number. Then spot the pattern that is formed. Be aware that the sequence may go forwards or backwards.

10) With LETTER SEQUENCES be aware that the letters can go forwards or backwards, either as single letters next to each other, or as pairs of letters.

11) If it is a multiple choice format 11+ test, make sure that you have put a line in every answer box on the answer sheet by the end of the test, especially if you can't work out the answer. Never leave an answer blank. You might still get a mark here.

12) If you do finish before the end, turn your pencil upside down and run it over the answer sheet checking that there are no missed out questions. Then if you have any time left, check through as much of the paper that you can for any mistakes you might have made.

APPENDIX 2 - USEFUL LINKS FOR THE 11+

In this chapter I have put together a list of 11+ links which may be helpful for parents wanting to know more about the subjects and topics discussed in this book. Please note that the author and Hadleigh Books cannot be responsible for the content and functionality of these websites.

11 Plus websites
The 11 Plus Website – www.the11pluswebsite.co.uk
11 Plus co uk – www.11plus.co.uk
11 Plus Eu - http://www.11plus.eu
11 Plus For Parents – www.11plusforparents.co.uk
11 Plus Guide – www.11plusguide.com
Eleven Plus Advice - www.elevenplusadvice.co.uk
Eleven Plus Exams – www.elevenplusexams.co.uk
On Line Eleven Plus Exams - http://onlineelevenplusexams.co.uk/

Revision websites
Activity Village - http://www.activityvillage.co.uk/
BBC Bitesize - http://www.bbc.co.uk/education
Bofa – www.bofa11plus.com
Education Quizzes – www.educationquizzes.com
Key Stages On Line – www.ksol.co.uk
MW Educational – www.mweducational.co.uk
11 Plus Swot – www.11plusswot.co.uk
You Tube – www.youtube.com/11plus

11 Plus/Education based forums
www.elevenplusexams.co.uk/forum/11plus
www.11plusguide.com/11-plus-forum
http://www.mumsnet.com/Talk/education

Tutoring websites
1st Tutors - https://www.firsttutors.com/uk/
Bright Young Things – www.brightyoungthings.co.uk
Find Good Tutors - www.findgoodtutors.com
Select My Tutor - http://www.selectmytutor.co.uk/
Tutorfair - https://www.tutorfair.com/
Tutors From Schools - https://www.tutorsfromschool.com/

Tutor Hunt - www.tutorhunt.com

Local Education Authorities
You Gov - http://local.direct.gov.uk/LDGRedirect/Start.do?mode=1
Schools Directory - http://www.alltheschools.com/lea.htm
Schools web directory -
http://www.schoolswebdirectory.co.uk/localauthorities.php

Grammar Schools
The National Grammar Schools Association - http://www.ngsa.org.uk/
Birmingham Consortium - http://www.birminghamgrammarschools.org/
Essex Consortium - http://www.csse.org.uk/
Lincolnshire Consortium – http://grammarschools.lincs.sch.uk/home/
Shropshire, Walsall & Wolverhampton Consortium –
http://www.qmgs.walsall.sch.uk/_content/admissions/2015_3_consortium
_information_leaflet.pdf
Slough Consortium - https://www.sloughconsortium.org.uk/
South West Hertfordshire Consortium -
http://www.swhertsschools.org.uk/

School Information websites
Boarding schools:- http://www.sbsa.org.uk/
Free Schools - https://www.gov.uk/types-of-school/free-schools
http://www.newschoolsnetwork.org
Independent schools - http://www.isc.co.uk/
Schools Net - http://www.schoolsnet.com/
Schools Web Directory - http://www.schoolswebdirectory.co.uk/
The Good Schools Guide - https://www.goodschoolsguide.co.uk/
The School Guide - https://www.schoolguide.co.uk/

Parents websites
BBC - http://www.bbc.co.uk/schools/parents/
Mums Net - http://www.mumsnet.com/
Net Mums - http://www.netmums.com/
Parents In Touch - http://parentsintouch.co.uk

Other relevant websites
The Advisory Centre for Education - http://www.ace-ed.org.uk/

Gifted and Talented Children - http://www.potentialplusuk.org/
Home Education - https://www.gov.uk/home-education
www.home-education.org.uk
www.electivehomeeducationservice.co.uk
www.heas.otg.uk
Hummingbird Books - http://www.hummingbirdbooks.co.uk/
League Tables for Schools -
http://www.education.gov.uk/schools/performance/
Mensa - http://www.mensa.org.uk/gifted-talented/children
Ofsted - https://www.gov.uk/government/organisations/ofsted
The Education Website – www.theeducationwebsite.com

Also by Mark Chatterton:-

The Student's Guide to English

This book has been compiled by an experienced teacher as an aid to learning the rules of English. It is suitable for both children and adults as a support to their English studies. It includes the topics of Punctuation, Parts of Speech, Grammar, Spelling, Comprehension and Writing. It can be used as a valuable revision tool for exams such as the 11+, the Common Entrance and GCSE exams, as well as for TEFL.

PDF E-BOOK FOR A PC –   ISBN 978-1-910811-00-9
MOBI E-BOOK FOR A KINDLE –   ISBN 978-1-910811-00-6
E.PUB E-BOOK FOR AN I PAD –   ISBN 978-1-910811-02-3

The Student's Guide to Mathematics

This book has been compiled by an experienced teacher as an aid to learning the rules of Mathematics. It is suitable for both children and adults as a support to their Mathematical studies. It includes the topics of number, calculations, money, shape, time, graphs and problem solving. It can be used as a valuable revision tool for exams such as the 11+, the Common Entrance and GCSE exams.

PDF E-BOOK FOR A PC –   ISBN 978-1-910811-05-4
MOBI E-BOOK FOR A KINDLE –   ISBN 978-1-910811-06-1
E.PUB E-BOOK FOR AN I PAD –   ISBN 978-1-910811-07-8

Both books are available from: www.hadleighbooks.co.uk

Printed in Great Britain
by Amazon